REMINISCENCES OF
A PORTRAIT PAINTER

Library of American Art

REMINISCENCES OF
A PORTRAIT PAINTER

By George P. A. Healy

Kennedy Graphics, Inc. • *Da Capo Press*
New York • *1970*

This edition of *Reminiscences of a Portrait Painter*
is an unabridged republication of the first edition
published in Chicago in 1894.

Library of Congress Catalog Card Number 78-96439

SBN 306-71829-4

Published by Kennedy Graphics, Inc.
A Division of Kennedy Galleries, Inc.
20 East 56th Street, New York, N.Y. 10022

and

Da Capo Press
A Division of Plenum Publishing Corporation
227 West 17th Street, New York, N.Y. 10011

REMINISCENCES

OF

A PORTRAIT PAINTER

GEORGE P. A. HEALY.

REMINISCENCES

OF

A PORTRAIT PAINTER

BY

GEORGE P. A. HEALY

CHICAGO

A. C. McCLURG AND COMPANY

1894

CONTENTS.

——◆——

PART I.

A Sketch of my Life.

PART II.

My Friends and my Sitters.

LIST OF ILLUSTRATIONS.

———◆———

List of Illustrations.   ix

Part I.

A SKETCH OF MY LIFE.

REMINISCENCES

OF A

PORTRAIT PAINTER.

———◆———

PART I.

A SKETCH OF MY LIFE.

IT would be a good thing, perhaps, if every man who had lived many years, who had been thrown in contact with interesting people, and had seen many phases of public and private life, would tell his story as simply as possible, and especially the story of his youth. I certainly do not believe that one man's experience can ever replace the personal experience of other men. Each generation is a little suspicious of the generations which have preceded it, and is determined to go its own way at its own risks and perils, perchance stumbling at times, but quite convinced that each stumble is a step forward.   But the story of a life made up of struggles, of hopes and fears, of defeats and victories, may be of some use in so far as it teaches a lesson of hope and courage. I shall, for my part, make the story a short one.   I have been a hard worker all my life.   Outside of his work a very busy man has but few events to relate.

My grandfather was an Irishman who was ruined by the rebellion of 1798. Being poor, naturally, he had a large family.   All he could do for his sons was to give fifty pounds to each of them, to wish them well, and to bid them henceforth provide for their own wants.   My father went to London, and was lucky enough to become a midshipman in the East India Company's navy. When his captain died, he went over to Boston, and was appointed captain of a merchant vessel, putting into the venture all his small earnings, and becoming before long a thorough American. He was a bold-spirited, imprudent man, excellently well fitted for the adventurous life he led. During the war with Tripoli, finding that his vessel was on the point of being captured by a corsair's craft, he caused all his men to land, remained himself till the last moment, blew up the ship, and barely escaped with his life. In 1812 he commanded another merchant vessel; all he possessed was invested in its cargo. An English privateer captured the ship, and sent its captain a prisoner to the island of Antigua.

Before starting on this ill-fated journey, my father had fallen in love with a mere child of fifteen, Miss Mary Hicks. He wrote to release her, but she refused to break her engagement; and when he was exchanged soon after, he returned to Boston, and married without much thought for the future. My father was not suited for a landsman's life; he was a sailor and nothing but a sailor, and each of his subsequent ventures proved disastrous.

I was the eldest of five children, and was born in Boston, July 15, 1813.

In those early days there was but little encouragement to artistic vocations, and certainly, as a small urchin, I should have been much surprised had any one predicted my future career. However, one of my early remembrances is of having caught a glimpse of our great painter Stuart. He had painted a portrait of my father before his marriage, so that the name was familiar to me. One day, as I was playing at marbles with some other boys of my age, one of them exclaimed: "There goes old Stuart!" I looked up; but all I saw of "old Stuart" was his back.

My grandmother, Mrs. Hicks, painted quite prettily in water-colors, and one of my delights as a child was to turn over a series of sketches she had made during a journey among the West Indian Islands. It is doubtless from her that I inherited my first liking for painting. Still, nothing in my early childhood seemed to indicate that I was to become an artist. I attended the public school, like all my companions, and my one idea was to earn a little money so as to help my mother. Life was not easy to the poor woman, with her growing family and her scanty and uncertain means. She had been a very pretty girl, of the frail, delicate American type; but anxiety soon caused her beauty to fade, and made her appear older than she was.

I must have been quite a small child when I began to understand the state of things at home, and to trouble my brains as to the best means of being

mother's right-hand man. American
boys are ready and willing to do anything in order to turn an honest penny,
from clearing the snow off rich people's
door-steps to sweeping a merchant's
store for him, — at least they were in
my day, and thought none the less of
themselves for their hard work. One
day I saw a gentleman get down from
his horse, and then look about him :
"Shall I hold your horse for you, sir?"
said I, not without some trepidation, for,
as a child, and even as a young man, I
was terribly timid. "Certainly, my boy ;
walk him up and down gently." I can
still see myself holding on firmly to the
reins, and pacing up and down the street.
Perhaps the gentleman was paying a visit
to his sweetheart, for it certainly proved
to be a long visit. When at last he
came out of the house, he was doubtless
amused by my eagerness to do my very
best in my important duty, for he gave

me a whole dollar. I do not know if, in my life, I have ever been much happier than when I rushed home in a state of wild excitement and threw the dollar into my mother's lap.

With her frail look and delicate health, she must have been a very energetic woman. It is to her that I owe not having been a cripple all my life. When I was about twelve years of age, I caught cold in my left leg, and the bone exfoliated. The muscles were so contracted that the doctors decided that amputation was necessary. One day my mother bade me straighten out the leg as much as I could, then suddenly she sat upon it, weighing down as much as she could. I screamed with the excruciating pain, and then fainted. But I did not lose my leg, and I have never even been lame since. Later, my mother said that the impulse which led her to do this was so strong that she could not have re-

sisted it; she seemed merely an instru
ment obeying some will stronger than
her own.

The first time that I held a brush
was when I was about sixteen years
of age. One day I was to meet a
friend of mine at his house, and we
were then to go off together on some
excursion. But as it began to rain
violently, I found my friend and his
two sisters amusing themselves with a
paint-box. They made drawings which
they afterwards colored. One of the
little girls, holding up her work where
bright reds, greens, and blues vied with
each other, exclaimed: " You could not
do as much, could you, George?" " I
guess I could," said I in true Yankee
fashion; and, nettled, I began to color
one of the childish drawings on which
the little girl obligingly wrote directions
as to the tints I should use. When I
had finished, my friends declared that

I must have painted before. But I had not. I had shown at school much aptitude for map drawing, but that was the first time I had ever used a brush.

After that, however, I would do nothing else. I determined to be a painter. In those days there were neither academies nor drawing-classes, nor collections of pictures to be studied. I began by copying all the prints I could find, by making likenesses of all who would consent to sit to me. The first useful thing I did was to paint a portrait of our butcher. That ought to have softened the opposition of my family, as doubtless much of the beef and mutton he had provided was still unpaid for. But parents then, if not now, looked with disfavor on artists, poets, and other such irregular persons! My grandmother, forgetful of her own artistic attempts, would shake her head as she looked at my daubs, and exclaim: "My poor George!

you will never be an artist; you will never make salt to your porridge!"

But in spite of all I persevered. When once my artistic vocation was made clear to me, I never hesitated a moment, I never looked back.

My first small success came to me in rather an odd way. Miss Stuart, who took some interest in me, lent me a print of Guido Reni's "Ecce Homo." I copied this on a canvas, and then colored it as best I could, without any help except such as the study of my own face afforded for the flesh tints. Such as it was, I carried the picture to a good-natured bookseller, who consented to put it in his shop-window. I own that I often found an excuse for passing along that street, so as to give a rapid glance at my work. In later years I have never seen an artist hover about his picture at a public exhibition without thinking of my "Ecce Homo" in the friendly bookseller's window.

ABRAHAM LINCOLN.

A Catholic priest from the country happened to pass that way, and stopped to look at the picture. Catholic priests are not rich now; in those days they were terribly poor. After hesitating, he went in and asked whether that picture was for sale. My friend the bookseller must have had a twinkle in his eye, as he answered that doubtless the artist would consent to part with his work — for a consideration. "I am not rich," said the priest; "all I could scrape together would be ten dollars." "I will speak to the artist, and give you an answer to-morrow." And on the morrow the priest carried away the "Ecce Homo," and the "artist" pocketed the ten dollars. I do not know which was the happier of the two; but I rather fancy it was the boy painter!

Some thirty years later, as I stood talking with some friends at the Capitol in Washington, I saw an old man wearing a Roman collar. On hearing my name pronounced by one of my friends he came up to me and said: "Are you Mr. Healy, the painter?" I bowed, and he continued with a smile: "I believe that I am the happy possessor of one of your earliest works, if not the earliest. Do you remember an 'Ecce Homo' which you had placed in the window of a Boston bookseller? A country priest offered ten dollars for it. I am that priest, and your picture still hangs in my little church. Who knows? it perhaps brought down blessings on your head. I have always felt that I had something to do with your success in life!" I shook my first patron heartily by the hand, and told him what joy his ten dollars had given me. But somehow, in the confusion of the moment, I neglected to ask him for his name and address. I have always regretted this. I should greatly have liked to pay him a visit, and see how my copy of Guido Reni looked in the Yankee country church.

The first serious encouragement which I received came to me from Sully, who, when I was about eighteen, was called to Boston to paint a portrait of Colonel Perkins for the Athenæum. Miss Jane Stuart, daughter of the great painter, spoke to him of "little Healy's" attempts, and he sent word to me that if I would make a sketch from Nature and a copy of one of Stuart's heads he would be glad to give me some advice. When I showed him what I had done, he looked at the canvases and exclaimed heartily: "My young friend, I advise you to make painting your profession!"

Seven years later, Sully was in London, having been sent there by the St. George's Society to paint a portrait of the Queen. I was also there, engaged on a portrait of the celebrated naturalist,

Audubon. I showed him my work as I had shown him my sketches, and after looking a long time in silence at the portrait, he said, with the courtly politeness for which he was noted : " Mr. Healy, you have no reason to regret having followed the advice I gave you some years ago."

It is a pleasure to me, after something like half a century to pay my debt of gratitude to this good painter, who was also so kindly a man and so thorough a gentleman. His portraits of women were peculiarly sweet and delicate, and in his day he was very popular. But an artist's reputation is a thing of fashion, of caprice also. Sully lived to be an old man; younger artists with different ideas and aspirations had sprung up by his side; little by little the popular painter grew to be less admired; his studio was nearly deserted; he was not a rich man, having through bad investments, I believe, lost a part of his earnings. Every time I went to Philadelphia I never failed to visit my old friend, and each time I found the same courteous and gentle-mannered man who first encouraged me; never complaining, glad that I had succeeded in life, as free from envy as though his own popularity had not waned, — a living proof that if some artists in the struggle to the front forget at times not only charity but even simple courtesy, others remain gentlemen even in the distress neglect brings with it. The noble and simple old man preached a lesson, by his very silence and dignity, which I have endeavored never to forget.

In the autumn of 1831, encouraged by Mr. Sully, I ventured to hire a painting-room, or what could pass for such, in the house of the late Richard Tucker, in Federal Street, Boston. I was then eighteen, and very determined to make my way in the world.   I was the happy possessor of an easel, paint-brushes, and canvases, and I nailed outside my door a board with my name and profession printed in very big letters. All I needed to make me perfectly happy was a sitter. Unfortunately the big sign failed to attract one; and though I painted my own portrait with a student's cap jauntily perched on one side and my beardless face treated as spiritedly as possible, I was not much richer when rent-day came around than if I had remained idly twirling my thumbs.

Having no money to give Mr. Tucker, I went frankly to him and told him about my trouble.   I felt sure that some day I should have sitters; but unluckily that day had not come.   Mr. Tucker smiled and said kindly: " You shall at least have a fair chance; paint me a portrait of my son Charles, and one of my son-in-law John H. Gray.   Who knows?   This first

commission may bring others in its wake.
Till then, don't let the rent trouble you!"
I do not know whether I was more fortunate than other beginners, but I seemed
always, when things were turning against
me, to find some kind hand stretched out
to help me. These two portraits are the
first I ever exhibited, and they attracted
some attention.

At this same exhibition I saw a very
charming portrait of a lady by Sully, —
it was that of his wife; and from that
time I had no peace. I had so far
painted only men; my ambition now was
to paint a woman's portrait, a beautiful
woman's portrait! I could think, dream
of nothing else. I was then painting
Lieutenant Van Brunt, and to him I
opened my heart. Ah! if I could but
have a lady sitter! He said: " Go and
call on Mrs. Harrison Gray Otis ; tell her
you want to paint her portrait, and that I
sent you."

Mrs. Otis was then the queen of fashion in Boston society. Her house was very popular, her entertainments celebrated, her sayings quoted, her beauty and elegance acknowledged by some, discussed by others. To be received by Mrs. Harrison Gray Otis was a sign that one belonged to " society," to the " right set ; " and in Boston, then as now, it was necessary to belong to the " right set."

I knew all this somewhat vaguely, as a mere boy, who by no means belonged to the famous " right set." I was distressingly timid. When I affirm that I am still timid, people are apt to laugh at me, and it is certain that having been thrown in contact with many different " sets," still more exalted than the Boston " upper ten " of 1832, I have conquered much of this painful timidity. But at nineteen years of age this shyness was terribly real, and at times caused me almost physical suffering.

ULYSSES S. GRANT.

I can still see myself going up the steps of Mrs. Otis's house. I held the knocker in my hand, then let it go, and ran for my life! But another time I screwed up my courage and saw the door open before me. I managed to ask the servant for Mrs. Otis ; I bade him say that " a gentleman wished to see her on business." Then, in mortal terror, I awaited her entrance. I dared not look at her, but with a sort of boldness which is sometimes the result of excessive timidity, I told her that I was an artist; that my ambition was to paint a beautiful woman, and that I begged her to sit to me.

Perhaps no woman is offended at a youth's blunt homage. Mrs. Otis was not ; she laughed out loud, showing her very pretty teeth. Then, growing serious once more, she asked to whom she was to have the honor of sitting. I had quite forgotten to introduce myself, and to men-

tion Lieutenant Van Brunt.   In spite of
this irregular sort of beginning to our
acquaintance, Mrs. Otis was probably
amused and perhaps interested, for she
called on me the very next day, and examined the portraits which I had already finished.   She seemed well enough
pleased, but I dared not speak again of
my ambitious hopes.   It was she who,
when I presented myself once more at
her house, awkward and speechless with
terror, said with a smile, " Well, Mr.
Healy, when shall I sit to you? "

This, my first portrait of a woman, was
a very audacious one.   I painted Mrs.
Otis laughing,—a thing which, had I had
more experience, I should perhaps not
have dared to do.   But her laugh was
charming, and she was fond of showing her perfect teeth and her dimples.
While I was preparing my colors she
glanced over the morning papers, and
in one of these was a sharp attack against

herself; this so amuscd her that she laughed heartily, and I was so struck by her charming face that I at once made up my mind to fix that laugh of hers on my canvas.

From that time " Little Healy," as people called me, became known. Mrs. Otis proved a warm-hearted friend and a very powerful one, and I was able not only to pay my rent to my patient landlord and my other expenses, but to help toward the support of my family.

I was, however, quite aware that, in spite of great natural facility, I had still everything to learn. I had had no master; what I knew I had acquired by dint of hard work, with the occasional advice of some older artist, but with no serious training. My one object was to become a student in a regular art school. But this could only be accomplished after I had scraped together not only money enough to take me to Europe and to help toward my support there, but to leave a sufficient sum with my mother to support her for a year or two, until I should be able to earn something on the other side of the big ocean. At last I was able to do this.

In the month of April, 1834, I secured my passage in a sailing-vessel called the "Sully." In those days one had to await a favorable wind before venturing out to sea. While I was thus waiting in New York, I called on Professor Morse, to whom I had a letter of introduction. This was just about the time when he was beginning to work out his discovery, the electric telegraph. Mr. Morse had been a painter; fortunately for the world he was something else besides. Doubtless he did not remember his career as a painter with pleasure, for he said to me somewhat bitterly,—

"So you want to be an artist? You won't make your salt, — you won't make your salt!"

" Then, sir," answered I, " I must take my food without salt."

This was the same prediction as my grandmother's. But I preferred to think of the encouragement I had received from Mr. Sully and others; and on the whole they were in the right.

A violent storm drove our vessel very rapidly toward France, and we were within two hundred miles of Havre in eight days after our sailing; but it required twelve more to accomplish the rest of the voyage.

I knew no one in France, I was utterly ignorant of the language, I did not know what I should do when once there ; but I was not yet one-and-twenty, and I had a great stock of courage, of inexperience, — which is sometimes a great help, — and a strong desire to do my very best. Thus everything amused and delighted me, — the peasant-women in their white caps, the noisy

market-places, the little urchins who in
the streets called out to each other in
French, that mysterious tongue! I was
soon in Paris, looking about me.

I had hoped to meet Mrs. Otis there;
but to my great disappointment she had
already left for Switzerland. Another
disappointment awaited me. Like all
Americans of that day, my interest was
centred in the Marquis de La Fayette;
to me he seemed to personate France:
he was then dying.

I at once entered the atelier of Baron
Gros, and went to work with a will, doing
my best to understand my master and
my comrades, and quickly catching up
enough French to make my way.

Gros was then a very fine-looking
man of sixty-three. His career had been
a most brilliant one, and yet he was far
from happy. Highly sensitive, almost
morbidly so, he suffered pangs from
things that a stronger man would have

despised. He had painted in the early years of the century his magnificent picture of the " Plague at Jaffa," now in the Louvre. He was recognized as one of the first among the French artists of his day. When the Bourbons once more returned to power, the painter of Napoleon's campaigns, instead of being out of favor, received important commissions and the title of baron. When I entered his atelier, he was still highly respected; but he was a saddened and almost despairing man. The influence of his master David was so strong upon him that, instead of following his own inspirations and painting spirited pictures of contemporary life, he endeavored to return to the old classical compositions, freezingly correct, such as he had admired in his youth. In this attempt he failed, and his later pictures are very inferior to those of his prime. Then he was a retiring man, or rather, perhaps,

he cared but little for the society which
others courted, was rarely seen outside
of his studio, and was not even sociable,
it is said, in his own family. He brooded
over the criticisms which, as time went
on, became more and more violent; each
pin-prick seemed to pierce the already
bleeding heart. The new school with
its violence, its innovations, its extrava-
gances, also found him a severe and
saddened outsider; everything seemed
to contribute to the darkening of his
latter days. One of the art critics exclaimed, "Gros est un homme mort!"
And Gros, as he received one of his intimate friends, said to him bitterly : " Ah !
you have come to see the dead man in
his tomb."   However, when the news
came of the suicide of another painter,
Leopold Robert, he was heard to say ;
"An artist ought never to kill himself;
he can never be sure of having done all
he was capable of doing."

WILLIAM TECUMSEH SHERMAN.

But on the 25th of June, 1835, Gros went to Bas Meudon, a little outside of Paris, and stretched himself on the sandy bed of the Seine, where there was but a depth of about three feet of water. Such was the miserable end of a man who had had, one might say, more than his share of success and glory. He had outlived his popularity, and his heart was broken.

My life at this time was a life of extreme sobriety and very hard work. I was full of respect for the dollars I had brought with me, and my noonday meal often consisted of a small loaf with fruit, or cheese when there was no fruit. But I had good health, high spirits, and immense pleasure in the progress I felt I was making day by day. I speak elsewhere of my journey to Italy in 1834, in company of chance acquaintances who became in time the best of friends, Sir Arthur and Lady Faulkner. From an artistic point of view, this first acquaintance with the marvels of the Italian galleries was the best of lessons.

In the spring of 1836 I went to London for the first time. I there exhibited a portrait of Mr. Francis Place, a great friend of Burdett and Bentham; and the portrait was liked. Joseph Hume, the radical Member of Parliament, wrote to me that if he could hope to have as good a portrait of himself he would willingly sit to me.

This letter followed me to France. I had undertaken, with two young French artists, a walking tour through France and Switzerland. This is one of my most delightful remembrances, though it was rough sort of travelling. We often walked twenty or thirty miles in one day, without being sure of finding food on the way; in out-of-the-way places we were glad at night to be allowed to throw ourselves down in some peasant's barn, with straw by way of beds, and to find a bowl of milk and some black bread for our breakfast. But we were free to go where we chose, to stop as long as we liked in picturesque nooks and sketch to our heart's content; we were young and strong, and very merry.

On one occasion a gentleman stopped to look at our work, and began to talk with us in the friendly way which is now much less the fashion in France than it used to be. English notions have invaded even the French provinces, and strangers, until they are "presented" to each other, hesitate to compromise their dignity by speaking. When I was a young fellow, this was by no means the case, and this conversation with an utter stranger seemed to us not only pleasant but perfectly natural. To the stranger it was evidently agreeable, for he said to us heartily: "I like artists; I have rarely the occasion of seeing any in this out-of-

the-way place. Will you give me the
pleasure of your company this evening
at dinner?" A real dinner, in a real
dining-room, with a host who could talk
of pictures and who appreciated artists!
Such a piece of good luck was not to be
despised, and the invitation was enthusi-
astically accepted. The stranger proved
to be a rich man who lived in a château,
and had an excellent cook as well as
an estimable cellar. I doubt whether he
ever gave a better dinner or a gayer
one.

It was in the midst of this journey
that I received Mr. Joseph Hume's letter, and I did not hesitate a moment to
retrace my steps. This was the beginning of my real career as an artist. I
describe my English experiences in a
separate chapter.

It was while I was at work in London
that I first met my wife. I had become
acquainted with a Mrs. Hanley, who one

day brought her young sister, Miss Louisa Phipps, to my studio. I met the ladies on the stairs as I was running to keep some engagement. I gave them the key of the room and excused myself. But this glimpse on the stairs was enough to fix my future destinies.

A miniature painter named Dubourjal, my dearest and best friend, had accompanied me to London. He asked permission to make a water-color drawing of this young girl. I still have the portrait. The costume of the day, with the high comb, the soft ringlets on either side of the face, the old dress, low-necked and with big puffed sleeves, — all this seemed to me, and seems to me still, perfectly charming. I followed the progress of the work with great interest, and somehow the young sitter was almost as often in my painting-room as in my friend's, — to that friend's great annoyance.

Twice the name of Dubourjal has come under my pen. I must stop a moment and pay a just tribute to that excellent friend, that loyal and faithful comrade. He was a few years older than I, a typical Frenchman, who never could get beyond a few broken English phrases; gay in spite of a rather hard life; the most unselfish and generous of men, happy at the success of others even when success did not come to him. The close friendship which united us continued after my marriage. Dubourjal was almost one of the family, knew all about our struggles, played with the children, and helped us out of more than one small difficulty.

Like many another imprudent young couple, we were given to entertaining our friends without exactly knowing how we should pay for the modest feasts. Our stock of silverware was of the smallest, but Dubourjal possessed a

M. DUBOURJAL.

dozen forks and spoons which he mys-
teriously brought in his coat-pocket on
gala nights. On one occasion he sent
us two bottles of particularly good wine.
He was proud of his knowledge of Bor-
deaux and Burgundy, without which no
dinner in France is complete. When
the wine was served, as it was with
great ceremony, each one of us held
his glass up to the light, admired the
fine red color of the wine, tasted it
with knowing looks, and declared it to
be delicious! A few days later the two
bottles, still corked, were found in a
closet. The servant, by mistake, had
given us the ordinary table wine. But
it did just as well.

In the summer of 1839 I was recalled
to France. I asked Miss Phipps whether
she would go with me, as my wife. We
had no time to make wedding preparations, and we were both too poor to
think of anything but our happiness;

which perhaps, after all, was not a bad
way of beginning life. I had already a
good connection, and was sanguine about
the future; but I had to provide for all
the wants of my family in America before thinking of my own: my parents
had both died since I left Boston, and
the education and support of my sister
and brothers fell upon me alone. My
marriage was therefore doubtless an ex-
traordinarily imprudent one. But a
folly can sometimes prove to be wisdom
itself.

We were married one morning at
the St. Pancras Parish Church, Euston
Road, London, assisted by three or
four friends only; my wife wore her
travelling-dress, for we started for Paris
as soon as the ceremony was over. I
shall never forget the look of pity which
the clergyman cast upon the bride. I
fear he did not consider me a respon-
sible sort of person. In those days a

mustache was worn only by soldiers or Frenchmen. I, therefore, with my un-shaven lip seemed to this respectable English clergyman a sort of Frenchman, which evidently was no recommendation; and my profession was not likely to make him less severe in his judgment. His glance said so plainly, " Poor child! " that I felt quite nettled.

It was with a hundred dollars in my pocket, by way of fortune, that I took my wife, who had not a penny of her own, to Paris. The journey was a hard one in those days; for after crossing the Channel, we got into a jolting *diligence*, where one had barely sitting room. And my bride was a sorry traveller! In spite of this unpropitious wedding-tour we be-gan life with perfect faith in each other and confidence in the future.

When I see young people, in our practical age, hesitate to marry because their means will not allow them to have

a fine house and every comfort from
the very first, I cannot help thinking of
our modest beginning in the Rue de
l'Ouest, now Rue d'Assas, near the Lux-
embourg Gardens. Attached to my painting-room there was a small bedroom, and
that was all our establishment. The *con-
cierge* kept the place clean, and we went
out for our meals. It was not a compli-
cated way of living; but it never struck
us that we were not the happiest mortals
under the sun.

Then our life was full of contrasts. I
had found an excellent friend in our
minister to Paris, General Cass, who
lived as a rich man and the representative of the United States should live.
As soon as he knew that I was married,
we were both invited to dinner. The question of dress — a very serious question —
arose. My wife was almost as inexpe-
rienced as myself on the subject. We
went together to the *Trois quartiers* on

the Boulevard, and chose white satin, to be covered with white crape; and this toilette proved to be deliciously fresh and pretty! The bride was very shy, all the more so because a tall footman was stationed behind her chair during the dinner, — a dreadful ordeal for her, — but the evening proved successful in every way. However, I was a little offended when Miss Isabelle Cass said to me: "You did not tell us that you had married a little girl!"

This contrast of the white satin gown and the establishment consisting of two rooms was a little symbolical of our life for many years thereafter. I was thrown by my profession in contact with people of high rank and large fortune; among those who became our friends, many were rich, and we, in spite of perhaps unusual good luck, struggled during all our youth at least, with our rapidly increasing family, against the difficulties

of life. This is, I think, one of the most
trying situations for people whose personal wants are modest, and who have
but one fear, — that of living beyond
their means.

A trifle will give an idea of our early
married life. We had moved to a rather
better place than that of the Rue de
l'Ouest, on the other side of the river;
the studio was larger, more fitted to receive distinguished sitters. We were both
tired of restaurant food, but still we did
not yet possess a kitchen and a cook, —
such luxuries, in our eyes, belonged to very
rich people indeed. But our big stove
boasted of something which might pass
for an oven, and Mrs. Healy one day
made up her mind to utilize this oven.
She bought a goose, and we rejoiced at
the thought of escaping that day from
the monotonous meal in an ill-ventilated
room, overcrowded with famished mortals. In due time the goose was shut
up in the oven.

The bell rang, and a gentleman entered. He was an important personage,
very rich, a possible sitter, one to be
well received by a struggling young
artist! I forgot all about the goose,
and showed my work to this amateur,
who seemed interested in it. He was a
prolix talker, and liked the sound of his
own voice. I insidiously encouraged this
weakness, and soon we were launched in
an interminable discussion on art,—art in
general, art in the past, art in America,
art everywhere. Our conversation was
accompanied soon by a low singing
sound, which soon became a sizzle, then
a veritable sputtering. The goose had
burst in upon the artistic talk. A strong
odor pervaded the painting-room, and a
glance convinced me of my wife's utter
wretchedness. But a well-primed talker
is not to be stopped by trifles. Once
or twice our visitor looked up a little
startled by the sputtering, and seemed

astonished at the strong odor; but I suppose he concluded that the kitchen was inconveniently near at hand, and the discussion went on. When at last the visitor left, we both rushed to the stove; the singing had ceased, the goose was little more than a cinder!

It was at the Salon of 1840 that I received for my portrait of Mrs. Cass a third medal, — the first public recompense accorded to me. I say elsewhere how the General, then our Minister to France, obtained for me sittings from the King, and how Louis Philippe later commissioned me to proceed to the United States to copy Stuart's Washington, and again to paint portraits of our great statesmen. After having been attracted to England, I now seemed fixed in France by the royal patronage, when in a moment the Revolution of 1848 changed all my worldly prospects. I had made frequent trips to America;

but always returned to France, where I
executed my two large pictures, "Webster replying to Hayne," and "Franklin
before Louis XVI.," which latter picture
won for me a gold medal at the Universal Exhibition of 1855. This was the
highest reward which had in those days
been granted to an American artist, and
gave me the right to send works to the
Salon without passing before the jury;
in other words, I became *Hors concours.*

I shall pass rapidly over this period
of my life. I was a hard worker, and
to a certain extent a successful one.
All my days were spent in my painting-
room; but I have always been fond of
society, and not infrequently we spent
the evenings with our friends. These
were nearly all Americans. The American colony in those days was smaller
than it is now, and less cut up into
various "sets;" the parties, the dinners
and teas, cordially offered were most

agreeable. It was not thought necessary to make a great display of wealth and fashion, to give jewels or costly trifles at the "çotillon," or to print the menu of a dinner on silver. Perhaps society was none the less pleasant for being more simple.

But, even then, there were Americans whom the French looked upon as people of fabulous wealth, sent by a kind Providence for the sake of needy noblemen in search of rich wives. Among these Colonel Thorn and his family held a distinguished position. Their house in town and their château in the country were thrown open with grand hospitality, and the "Colonel Torn"—the "th" being impossible to pronounce for the French — was popular among all the fashionables of the day. His table was highly appreciated, his horses well known; they were especially noted for their long flowing tails. The Colonel said to me with a twinkle

in his eyes: " They don't know that I
treat my horses' tails as women do their
back hair; I add on a switch!" The
Colonel was a remarkably handsome
man, and his numerous daughters were
nearly all beautiful. But the youngest
was the most perfect of all as to features.

I painted a portrait of this youngest
daughter, Miss Ida Thorn, then a very
young girl of about sixteen or seventeen.
I was also then painting an English
young lady, Miss Sneyde, whose beauty
was exciting great admiration in Paris.
I have always thought that these two
lovely girls represented most admirably
the beauty of their two countries. Miss
Sneyde, some years older than Miss Thorn,
less slight, beautifully formed, was a mar-
vel of color. Her hair was of that reddish gold tint that our belles sometimes
most foolishly try to acquire artificially,
and it waved naturally; the eyes were
blue, the lips very red, the skin almost

dazzlingly white. My American sitter's hair was nearly black, her eyes dark; the features were clean-cut and exquisitely delicate, the figure perfectly graceful. It would have been difficult to decide which was the more beautiful of the two; and the painter, glad not to be forced to choose, admired each more than the other, according to the sitter he was at the moment painting.

The days when we lived in two rooms and roasted a goose in the studio, were past. I managed to give every necessary comfort to my growing children, but the future was still uncertain. We had lost two of our elder children, both boys, and this was our only great sorrow; but others came with a regularity which filled our French acquaintances with amazement; and with every child our responsibilities increased. It was high time to think of ways and means.

A trifling incident changed the course

of my life. Among the Americans who
visited Paris somewhat before the Universal Exhibition of 1855 was William
B. Ogden, one of the "fathers" of the
young city of Chicago. I do not know
if, during my long career, I have ever
met a man of greater charm of manner.
The word "genial" seemed made for
him. Remarkably intelligent, very well
informed, a delightful talker, full of energy, of will, of originality, he seemed
destined by nature to be a leader. He
had, from the first, believed in the mar-
vellous future of the small town, where a
few years before there had stood but a
fort. His descriptions of the new city
fired my imagination. I had often
thought of returning to the United
States and settling there; but the difficulty of moving with a large family, the
uncertainty as to where I should go, the
fear of being considered by my country-
people, according to the frank saying of

one of them, as a " blasted foreigner," had
made me hesitate. Then, too, I had
been engaged on large works more easily
accomplished in Paris than elsewhere.
Now my second large picture was finished,
ready for the great exhibition, and I was
free to shape my course otherwise. Mr.
Ogden most warmly urged me to start
for Chicago, offering me the hospitality
of his house, promising his support, and
predicting success. I quickly made up
my mind, and in the autumn of 1855
started for Chicago, leaving my family
in Paris.

Chicago was then in a somewhat
rough stage. Like an overgrown youth
whose legs and arms are too long for
his clothes, and who scarcely knows how
to dispose of his lank, awkward body,
the city stretched along the lake shore
and out on the prairie, unfinished, rag-
ged, and somewhat uncouth as yet. The
streets were abominably paved ; the side-

WILLIAM B. OGDEN.

walks, raised high above the level of the streets, were composed of rough planks, often out of repair, so that one had to pick one's way carefully for fear of accidents; big nails seemed placed there on purpose to catch in the women's dresses, and as in those days the hideous fashion of crinoline, or "hoops" as they were called, had just reached the Far West, many were the falls occasioned by these nails. The mud was so deep in bad weather, that from side to side rickety boards served as unsafe bridges, and the unfortunate horses waded laboriously along as best they could. Chicago has changed somewhat since 1855!

And with it all, Chicago in those rough, far-away days was delightful. The wooded North side especially, where resided Mr. William B. Ogden and most of my other kind friends, well justified the name of " Garden City " which Chicago bore. Land had not then risen so much in price as to make a big space about each house an impossible luxury; the trees were magnificent, and in summer almost hid the houses one from the other. Mr. Ogden's house, kept by his sister and brother-in-law Mr. and Mrs. Edwin Sheldon, stood in the midst of a whole "block," — a large, roomy, comfortable, old-fashioned frame house, spreading broadly in the midst of the enormous garden, or "yard," as people modestly called their gardens, — the trees were superb, the flower-beds of the brightest hues, the lawn stretched before the house: it was a delightful residence, — a town house with the pleasant aspect of a country place.

And this may be taken as a typical house among the rich citizens of that day. Alas! the Fire has swept over Chicago of the olden time; the broad-spreading homesteads, the fine trees that had sheltered the games of Indian

children fifty years before, — all these
have disappeared. And it seems to
me the Fire destroyed more than the
homesteads, more than the gardens: it
destroyed the simplicity, the cheerful
kindliness, of a town still too young to be
arrogant. Chicago is now a superb city,
— the "representative American city,"
worthy to have been chosen for the glorious World's Fair. But somehow, even
in the midst of its magnificence, I sometimes regret the rough town where I was
so warmly welcomed toward the end of
1855. It is true that the most enormous
rats I ever saw held their noisy meetings
under the high wooden sidewalks, and
uncouth shanties raised their shabby
heads close to fine new mansions; but
then hospitality in the young city was very
charming, and its home circles were full
of kindly feeling and of high culture too.

In the wild race toward the most extraordinary fortune ever attained in so

short a time, even in our country, it will
not be a matter of surprise when I say
that land agents, merchants, and bankers
were more plentiful than artists in Chicago. I arrived therefore at an excellent
moment: prosperity was almost universal. The following year a terrible money
crisis put a momentary check to this prosperity, but in 1855–1856 every man felt
that he was rich or would soon be so. I
regret not having kept an account of the
portraits I painted during the first twelve
months of my sojourn in the Garden City.
But perhaps it is just as well, as I might
be taxed with exaggeration. I was then
in the full strength of my years, capable
of much fatigue, not dreaming that I
should later have to pay for this over-
straining of my nerves and this excess
of work.

One of my first pictures was a group
of Mr. Sheldon and his two young children, which became very popular. I am

glad of this opportunity of speaking not only of Mr. Ogden, whose guest I was during this first year, but also of Mr. and Mrs. Sheldon, who took me into their delightful home circle as one of their own, and whose friends became my friends. I never saw a more charming example of hearty American hospitality and kindliness.

It would be impossible for me to speak here of all the kind friends I made at this happy time. The old settlers welcomed and encouraged me: Mr. and Mrs. McCagg; Mr. Kinzie, of whose pretty and lively daughter I painted a large portrait; the Rumsey family; Dr. and Mrs. Brainard; many others besides. Lifelong friendships began for me then which neither time nor long absence could undermine.

Among the most successful portraits I painted at this time I can mention that of Mrs. Thomas B. Bryan, whose hospitable house was always open to me and mine.   Mr. Bryan and I agreed on many points, but the greatest bond of sympathy perhaps was our admiration for our respective wives, — for each other's wives too !

Even an artist — and every one knows how unfit such a man is for business operations — could not resist the " land fever " then raging in this new place. Fortunes were realized by clever speculators in a fabulously short time ; fortunes also were lost, but of those one heard less than of the first.   I was led to invest some of my earnings in a stretch of sand abutting on the lake and on the North side ; a deserted and desolate-looking place it was, which cost me for many a long year tax money, and brought in not a penny.   A time came when the investment proved to be a very good one ; but as I had a well-earned reputation for bad speculations,

MRS. THOMAS B. BRYAN.

that sand was often thrown into my eyes.

The sand might have run through my fingers, and with it all my prospects for peace and comfort in later years, but for the kindness of my best and dearest friend, Mr. E. B. McCagg. He fought for my rights when my claim to this property was contested, he cared for it and worked in my interest as he would scarcely have done in his own. Of all the boons Heaven bestows on poor humanity, few are more precious than that of a perfect friendship.

I confess that some of my investments were less fortunate. On one occasion, a few years later, one of my supposedly dear friends assured me that he was determined to make my fortune, as artists were quite incapable of enriching themselves. I was convinced of this humiliating fact, and duly grateful to this generous-minded benefactor. I gave

into his hands a goodly bundle of bank-
notes, and he, in exchange, gave me a
title-deed.   On my return to Chicago —
this brilliant transaction occurred in
Washington — I bethought me of my
investment, and asked to have it registered.   The clerk who was to attend to
the affair, and who knew me of old, said
compassionately, after having looked into
the thing· "But, Mr. Healy, it will cost
you something to have this registered, —
five dollars perhaps."   "Well, what of
that?"   "But the whole thing is not
worth five dollars."   "What?"   I could
not believe my ears.   If that was a way
of making my fortune, I was quite as
capable of improving my prospects as my
Washington friend.   The clerk explained
to me that the land sold really did exist,
but it was under the waters of the lake
instead of being on its banks.

I was so flattered, so delighted with
my Chicago reception that I sent for my

family; and in November, 1856, we settled in a tall frame house on Ontario
Street. The house was slightly built,
and a roaring furnace filled Mrs. Healy,
unaccustomed to American life, with
terror, lest the wooden house should burn
like a match. It did not escape its fate,
but it was after we left it.

As I have already said, the extraordinary prosperity of Chicago soon under-
went a sudden and violent check, and I
was not that year tempted to buy more
sand. But I have always been grateful
to have been led to fix my tent for a
number of years in Chicago, or rather
near Chicago, as in 1857 we moved into
the country for the sake of the children's
health. We were still settled at Cottage
Hill, now Elmhurst, — the elder children
at school, the younger ones running wild
like young colts, — when the war broke
out.

I happened to be in Charleston at this

time, engaged in painting a number of portraits, and I assisted in the wild excitement which ended in the bombarding of Fort Sumter. I had never mixed in politics, but I was a Northern man, with Northern feelings and antislavery principles. Like many others, I hoped that things might yet be peaceably arranged; and at any rate I was busy, and never thought of leaving my work on account of the threatening storm. But one of the Charleston papers informed the Yankee painter "that if he had not left the city before the sun went down, he should be tarred and feathered." My host read the article to me, and I burst out laughing; the thing struck me as merely ludicrous. But my Southern friend by no means laughed, but said: "A carriage shall be at the door in an hour, and you must leave town. Otherwise they would prove as good as their word."

This war-time was hard upon me; for

MR. & MRS. BRYAN'S LITTLE GIRL.

when bare necessities of life are obtained with difficulty, such luxuries as portraits are not to be thought of. This was especially true during the first part of this terrible war; later, if some were ruined, others made rapid fortunes, and speculation became as audacious as ever.

Among my sitters during these dreadful years, I counted many of our most celebrated generals, — Grant, Sherman, McClellan, Admiral Porter, and many others. I also had sittings from Abraham Lincoln. These I particularly enjoyed. So much has been said about that great and good man that it seems almost presumptuous to add to the numberless anecdotes of his humor and genial temper. During one of the sittings, as he was glancing at his letters, he burst into a hearty laugh, and exclaimed: " As a painter, Mr. Healy, you shall be a judge between this unknown correspondent and me. She complains of my ugliness. It is allowed to be ugly in this world, but not as ugly as I am. She wishes me to put on false whiskers, to hide my horrible lantern jaws. Will you paint me with false whiskers? No? I thought not. I tell you what I shall do: give permission to this lover of the beautiful to set up a barber's shop at the White House!" And he laughed again with perfect delight.

At the close of the war the idea came to me to paint a picture to be called " The Peacemakers." It represented Lincoln, Grant, Sherman, and Porter, on board the " River Queen," discussing the possibilities of peace. I made all the studies for this picture in America, but I painted it some years later in Rome. It was unfortunately burned in 1892, when the Calumet Club of Chicago was destroyed by fire.

We moved back to town in 1863, and I bought an old-fashioned house on

Wabash Avenue, which disappeared, with all it contained, in the Great Fire of 1871.

Social life, in spite of public events, went on much as usual, and our circle of intimate friends was still that in which I had been so kindly welcomed on my arrival.

But constant hard work was beginning to tell upon my health, on my nervous system especially. It was evident that as long as I remained in Chicago I should inevitably do more than my strength would permit. To refuse a commission was more than I could ever do! Finally, it became a vital question: I must force myself to rest, or the machine would give out before long. It was then that we took, not without much hesitation, the resolution of going abroad once more. We intended to stay a few years only; we did not return to Chicago until 1892. It is true that my previous visits to America had always been very frequent.

My strength had come back, thanks to moderation in work ; the grandchildren with their French accent were growing up, and it seemed almost impossible again to fold up our tent. But the desire to live among my own people grew within me as the years went on, and I am pleased to find myself once more in the American city I love best, which adopted me as its own in 1855, and welcomed me home so heartily in 1892.

As I look back upon my long life, as I think of the early years in Paris at the time when Gros killed himself, when Delacroix, that audacious young inno-vator, excited the anger and contempt of Ingres, when the landscapes of Corot were refused at the Salon, when my old and dear friend Couture was considered a revolutionary spirit not to be encour-aged by the authorities, I can but smile — a little sadly, perhaps — at the violence of the young men of our day, who in their turn will be looked upon as old fogies by the youths of thirty or forty years hence. And so the world goes on! Fashion changes; the beautiful of yesterday is the grotesque of to-day. What matters it? Each generation as it comes to life does its best, struggles, suffers, hopes, or despairs; it adds its little stone to the big edifice which is ever being built; the little stone is lost among others, forgotten, overlooked; but it has helped nevertheless to make the wall solid and beautiful. And that surely is something.

Part II.

MY FRIENDS AND MY SITTERS.

THOMAS COUTURE.

MY first meeting with Couture, who became one of my best and dearest friends, was odd and characteristic. It was in 1834; I was not yet one-and-twenty, and had just arrived from the United States. I was beginning to understand a few words of French, and had entered the studio of the great and unfortunate painter, Gros. If I understood but few of the things the master and pupils said to me, I understood the language of the pencil, and worked all the harder that I was more estranged.

One day, as the model was resting, and I was looking at my morning's work in a somewhat melancholy state of mind, a short, thick-set young man, with bright brown eyes and shaggy hair, unceremoniously pushed me aside, saying, " Donne-moi ta place, petit." I was going to protest, when I saw my fellow-student so absorbed that I grew interested in what he was doing. He coolly turned over my sheet of gray paper and sketched the model, who, resting, had fallen into a far better attitude than that which we had copied. The outline drawing was so strong, so full of life, so easily done, that I never received a better lesson. When he had finished, he left my place as coolly as he had taken it, seemingly quite unconscious of my existence.

I did not then know the name of this free-and-easy comrade, but I kept the drawing and prized it. I am sorry to say that the woman intrusted with the care of my room had but small respect for the fine arts, and being one

day in need of paper to light my fire,
took a number of drawings for that
purpose. Among those drawings was
the outline sketch by Thomas Couture.

I was scarcely able to profit much
by my illustrious master's directions.
As I have said elsewhere, Baron Gros,
unable to bear the loss of that popularity which had so long been his,
ended his life by throwing himself into
the Seine.

Gros's pupils dispersed, and I had no
opportunity to make further acquaintance with my eccentric fellow-student.

Some years later, when the estranged
boy that I was in 1834 had become a
young man, I happened to pass with a
comrade, — a young Englishman named
Toplis, — near the shop of Desforges, who
sold canvases and paints, and who also
exhibited pictures in his window. I was
greatly struck by a picture representing
a young Venetian, and endeavored to

excite my companion to enthusiasm. Toplis was hungry, and at first thought more of his delayed lunch than of the painting. But he soon forgot his hunger, and exclaimed: "By Jove! I must get my brother to buy that." Lucky fellow! I had a certain respect for a painter whose brother was rich enough to buy pictures. In those days painters were by no means able to build their own grand studios, and to fill them with wonderful draperies and precious bric-à-brac; as a usual thing, they belonged to modest families, who mourned over the son and brother who had embraced such a profession.

Mr. Toplis bought the picture signed "Thomas Couture," and paid the color-dealer a thousand francs for it. I afterward found out that the artist received only three hundred francs. As it happened, it was I who was commissioned to go to his studio. As soon as I entered

I saw that Couture was no other than the fellow-student who had so unceremoniously takén my place. I was so delighted at the coincidence that Couture, who naturally did not recognize me at all, thought me a little crazy. I exclaimed, " I am so glad that it is you! "

I must now confess a little weakness of mine. When I am excited and pleased by any unexpected event, I rather enjoy the bewilderment of those who are not in the secret. After all, each must find his pleasure where he can! But after a while Couture understood that I was not the rich amateur who had bought his picture, but only a poor devil of a painter like himself, and that we both had been pupils of Gros. Our friendship dated from that moment.

There was in Couture's talent such vigor, such frankness, so much of life and truth, that my admiration for the artist equalled my liking for the man.

He was apart among the painters of
the day; as far removed from the cold
academic school as from the new art,
just then making its way, with Delacroix
at its head. The famous quarrel between the classic and the romantic camps
left him indifferent. He was, even then,
of too independent a nature to follow any
chief, however great. He was — himself.
His great aim was to approach Nature
as near as possible, to give life and passion to his painted figures; and in that
he succeeded wonderfully.

On that first visit of mine to his bare
studio, — a very different-looking place
from the lovely boudoir-like studios
of fashionable painters nowadays, — I
saw him at work on a picture only just
sketched in. He exclaimed: "The amateur who will buy that canvas for a thousand francs will have his money's worth.
Don't you think so?" A thousand
francs! The picture was large, and

represented the prodigal son, a life-size figure. The young man, seated by the wayside, a goatskin about his loins his only garment, thin, his deep-sunken eyes full of despair, his brow overshadowed by a thick shock of black hair, seems to ruminate over his past follies and their consequences. In the background pass a man and a woman: the young woman is full of compassion, while her companion points to the prodigal and seems to tell his story. The contrast between the prodigal son and these lovers is very happily indicated; and the rich tones of the man's red drapery relieve the sombreness of the rest of the picture. While examining the sketch I said to my new friend: " My sitters pay me a thousand francs for a portrait. If you will allow me to pay you by instalments, I will be that amateur, and I offer you not a thousand francs, but fifteen hundred."

I was very proud of my purchase, but a little troubled too. In those days my sitters were not very numerous, and I borrowed of Mr. Toplis, the brother of my fellow-student, the first sum paid to Couture. But I never regretted this youthful folly of mine. " The Prodigal Son " remained in my studio for many years, and I took it with me to America. Finally, I gave it, with many other pictures, to the city of Chicago. I am sorry to say that the whole collection was destroyed in the Great Fire of 1871. A small sketch of " The Prodigal Son," and a most spirited one, still exists; it belongs to M. Barbedienne, the famous bronze-dealer, who was a personal friend of Couture, and possesses a number of pictures, drawings, and sketches by the master.[1]

Thomas Couture was of humble origin,

[1] Since this sketch was written, M. Barbedienne has died, and his collection belongs to his heirs.

and had to fight his way in life; he fought it bravely and successfully. He was born in Senlis, not far from Paris, on the 21st of December, 1815. Sturdy, thick-set, short, with a big voice and somewhat rough manners, he was by no means what is called a "lady's man." He never frequented society, and had a profound contempt for those who did. He was a great worker, — in his youth especially, for later he grew much fonder of his ease. He cared only for the life of the studio and for artists' jokes, and, I am sorry to say, practical jokes were his particular delight.

If he had not been a painter, he might have been a most inimitable comic actor. When he told a story, — and he told funny stories by the dozen, — he would act it; his face would turn and twist, his eyes would dance, his nose, with its peculiar nostrils opening upward, would sniff, and he managed so admirably to render the tone of voice and the gestures of those he imitated that he actually looked like them. I remember that, many years later, happening to speak of a very fussy old lady with whom we were both acquainted, and whom he had known when she was young, he so caught the twist of her head, the pleading of her eyes, the flattery of her society phrases, that I saw her before me, and not only as she was then, but as she must have been twenty or thirty years before.

Couture was a stanch and faithful friend. We were often separated, as I continually went to America or to England; but when I returned to Paris I was sure to find my old comrade such as he had been when we parted. When I married, and presented him to my young wife, the impression was not so favorable as I should have liked. His big, loud voice, his free-and-easy manners, and especially his practical jokes, which he did not always reserve for the painting-room, greatly disturbed the shy young Englishwoman. At one time he never came to dine with us without bringing in his pocket a tame lizard, which would run up his back and nestle against his neck, or would play the same trick with unsuspecting strangers. He did his best to inspire a disgust for oysters by showing the creatures to be living at the moment when they were swallowed. Many other such trifles were set down against him at first; but with time, and especially after his own marriage, these eccentricities were softened down, and his real sterling qualities — the good heart, the faithfulness, the sturdy courage, and the manly energy — grew to be more thoroughly appreciated.

These strong qualities did not go without a certain rough independence of

character which did not help him to success and official dignities. He divided
the world into two distinct classes: artists, — that is, those whom God created
to be the masters of the world, — and the
others, whom he called with infinite contempt " les bourgeois." The greatest
statesmen, kings, noblemen, or shopkeepers were all " bourgeois," — that is,
inferior beings, who should consider it an
honor to buy pictures or statues at the
highest possible rates. As to allowing
them the right of directing in any way
the artist they employed, that was not
to be thought of. Their first duty was
to be eternally satisfied, grateful, and
enthusiastic.

At the time that Guizot published his
work on Washington, I was commissioned by a group of Americans to paint
a portrait of the great statesman. The
sittings were most agreeable, and conversation between the painter and the sitter

never flagged. I happened to mention
Couture, and I spoke so warmly of my
fellow-student that Guizot expressed a
wish to see him. The picture of " The
Prodigal Son," which he had admired
during his sittings, proved to him that
my enthusiasm was not inspired merely
by friendship. We therefore went together to Couture's studio. He had
utilized one of his bare walls to sketch
in the picture which was to become so
celebrated under the title of " The Romans of the Decadence." Even in that
rough state it was easy to see what a
strong work it was, and the visitor was
very much struck by it. Guizot was then
all-powerful, and most painters would
have shown themselves more flattered
by this visit than did Couture ; he considered it but his due. When the statesman asked him whether he had no
order for this picture, he answered,
" J'attends." The orders should come

to him ; he would never run after them. Guizot smiled, but continued most graciously, —

" Who was your master ? "

" Delaroche."

After the death of Gros, Couture had entered Delaroche's atelier, but remained only a short time under a master whom he did not admire.

" M. Delaroche is a friend of mine," answered Guizot; " I shall have great pleasure in speaking of you to him."

And he evidently did speak to Delaroche of his pupil, for a short time after this visit Couture happened to meet his old master, the most successful artist of the day, the favorite painter of Louis Philippe and of all his family. Delaroche went up to him and said, —

" M. Guizot seems to have been struck by your work ; he told me so. I replied that you had been my favorite pupil, you had natural talent, but you have strayed from the true path, and I cannot recommend you."

Probably the favorite court-painter influenced his royal patrons, for when the " Decadence " was exhibited at the Louvre — in those days the " Salon " took place in the long gallery, the modern canvases hiding the works of the old masters — the King, Louis Philippe, when he visited the exhibition, managed to turn his back on Couture's picture, both in coming and in going. The painter's contempt for " bourgeois " taste by no means kept him from feeling this royal behavior most keenly. However, the picture had such great success, was so generally praised, suddenly causing its author to become famous in a day, that the State bought it for the very large sum of six thousand francs! This sudden reputation of his ex-pupil probably caused Delaroche to modify his judgment. At any rate, he called on Couture some time after the purchase of his picture, and said, —

"M. Couture, I have greatly disapproved, I still disapprove, of your conception of art, but I do not deny that you have talent. You have made for yourself a place in art; let us be friends."

But Couture was not a man to be taken by a few pleasant words; he drew back and answered,—

"M. Delaroche, you have had immense success, you are a member of the Institute, you have innumerable admirers. I never was, I never can be, among those admirers. Therefore there can be no question of friendship between us two."

And, bowing, he left the great man somewhat astonished at this manner of responding to his advances.

Couture was a good painter, but a very bad courtier; he proved it every time he was placed in contact with the great ones of this world, whether sovereigns or members of the Institute of France. That

was not the way to make his talent
popular. The rough independence of
his nature could admit of no sort of
compromise. He had several opportunities of making his way to honors and
to fortune, — opportunities which another
might have utilized, but which he wasted.
Doubtless he made good resolutions; but
when the time came he was unable to
control his impatience and his sharp
retorts.

If Louis Philippe did not appreciate
the painter of the " Decadence," his reputation was so well established when Napoleon III. took possession of the throne
that it was impossible to treat him slight-
ingly, though Couture's talent was not
such as courts, as a usual thing, care to
encourage. The favorite painter of the
Third Empire was Winterhalter, as Delaroche had been of the Orleans family.
However, an order was given to Couture
for a large picture representing the bap-

tism of the little Prince Imperial. He
went to work with great ardor, making
sketches and preparing a vast composi-
tion. In the course of the work, sittings from the various members of the
imperial family and their immediate fol-
lowers were granted to him. If a portrait-painter, when his sitters are ordinary
mortals, is often driven to the verge of
insanity, it is easy to judge how his
temper is tried and his nerves unstrung
when those sitters are princes or sovereigns. It is likely that in Couture's case
the sittings were not agreeable either to
the painter or to his models. Napoleon
III. wished to direct his artist, and of all
artists Couture was the least easy to
direct. Finally, one day, goaded beyond
endurance, the painter turned around and
said : " Sire, who is to paint this picture,
— your Majesty or I ? " And neither
painted it ! The Emperor gave no more
sittings, turned his back on the painter,

and his courtiers turned theirs also. The order was not maintained, and all the work of many months was wasted.

Couture never recovered from this bitter disappointment. He shook the dust from his feet, and returned contempt for contempt. From that day on he never sent any work to the annual Salon, and, little by little, so retired from the world that many thought him dead. For many of his contemporaries he remained the painter of the " Decadence," as though he had painted only that one picture. How many times have I not heard young painters exclaim : " Couture — ah, yes, Couture of the Romans. But he died ages ago, or, if he still vegetates somewhere, he must be very old indeed. No one has heard of him for many a long year ! " In reality, when Couture died, in March, 1879, he was not sixty-four years of age.

The truth is that Couture never ceased

working, though he worked after a somewhat irregular fashion, giving himself numerous holidays. If he was neglected by the great mass of his countrymen, he was appreciated elsewhere. One of his most charming works, " The Falconer," of which I made a copy the size of the original, is in Germany. But most of his pictures were bought, I am glad to say, by Americans. It is rather odd that the " nation of shopkeepers," as ours is often termed, should have a love of art and the instinct of the real amateur more fully developed than many an Old World country. When Millet was still, if not unknown, at least violently criticised in France, America already possessed some of his best works ; Barye found his most fervent admirers in the United States ; Couture painted almost exclusively for Americans.

Couture married rather late in life, and had two children, both girls. He was adored by his wife and daughters, and his married life was a very happy one. Perhaps, with our ideas on such matters, we might consider that his theory of the superiority of the male creature, and his right to absolute devotion on the part of his womenfolk, was a reprehensible theory. But he made an excellent father and husband in spite of his conviction that a man was not made to be faithful to one woman, and that education for girls was a dangerous modern notion, not to be encouraged by a reasonable man.

In 1869 he purchased a country place at Villiers-le-bel, a short distance from Paris. The house dated from the time of Francis I., and the garden, or rather park, was filled with grand old trees. Here he resided during the last ten years of his life, going to Paris only during a few months in winter. His peculiar ideas of happiness caused him to live in what other mortals might consider

great discomfort.   Under pretext that
Nature managed things for the best, he
never allowed a gardener to work on his
grounds.   He was, besides, quite convinced that such hirelings made it a
point to sell his vegetables and to steal
his fruit.   As a natural consequence the
beautiful place went to ruin ; the trees
brought forth no fruit, and the earth
yielded no vegetables.   He himself took
great delight in wearing peasant's gar-
ments and in walking in *sabots*, — they at
least had nothing to do with civilization !
But as he had a thorough appreciation of
the delights of a good table, he employed
an excellent cook, and his devoted wife
took care that his meals should be of the
best and his truffles of the largest.   But for
the rest of the service a village girl was
quite sufficient, and he deemed it by no
means beneath the dignity of his wife and
daughters to perform domestic duties of
the most active sort.

In his country retreat he was not, however, abandoned. Pupils gathered about him, living in the village so as to profit by the master's advice. Among these were many Americans. Mr. Ernest Longfellow, son of the poet, was of the number. Couture was an excellent master, and took great interest in the progress of his pupils. His great precept was, "Look at Nature; copy Nature." He published a little book full of good advice to young artists, giving the result of many years' experience. All his pupils were fond of him, which proves that the exterior peculiarities, which sometimes shocked strangers, were soon overlooked by those who were able to appreciate his sterling qualities. A man who is loved by the members of his family, to whom all his friends remain faithful, and who is appreciated by young people, is sure to be of a thoroughly lovable nature.

Still, it must be owned that the first

impression was not always quite agreeable. On one occasion an American, a
rather shy and exquisitely polite gentleman, and a great admirer of Couture's
talent, went, provided with a letter of
introduction, to pay his respects to the
master. The master was in his bath; but
when his wife told him of the visit, " Let
him come in!" exclaimed he; and, much
to our countryman's confusion, he was
received by Couture, soaking placidly in
his bath. He rather splashed his visitor,
for, like many Frenchmen, he gesticulated
freely while conversing.

Couture was fond of telling the story
of his first pupil. He was still a young
man when, one morning, he heard a timid
knock at his door. " Come in!" said he,
in that big, gruff voice of his, scarcely
calculated to encourage shy visitors. A
young fellow, slightly deformed, dressed
like a well-to-do countryman, entered,
and, not without much hesitation and

much stuttering, begged the painter to take him in as pupil. " I have no pupils, and I wish for none," was the discouraging answer. But the youth, if he was timid, was tenacious; he would be so discreet; his master need not feel his presence; all he asked for was a corner of the atelier from which he could see the great artist at work; he would make himself of use, wash the brushes, set the palette, run errands, — do anything, in short, that was required of him. Couture continued to say no; the young man continued to plead. Finally the artist impatiently took up his pipe and found that his tobacco-pouch was empty. " Go and buy me some tobacco!" he cried. The young man disappeared, and soon returned; Couture smoked, was mollified — and yielded.

This strange pupil remained with him for more than a year. Couture often wondered how he managed to live. He seemed poor, but he never borrowed money. He spent all his time working, without showing very great natural talent, and Couture's excellent heart was much concerned. How was that poor fellow ever to get salt for his porridge with his painting?

One day the pupil begged a great favor of his master, — to let him invite him to dinner. Couture consented; and, to his amazement, the young man, dressed like a gentleman, took him to the best restaurant in Paris, and ordered the best dinner that restaurant could provide.

The poor, humble pupil who ran on his errands and washed his brushes was a very rich amateur, whose passion for painting had led him to seek the sincere and disinterested lessons of a master he admired. Later, Couture went to visit his ex-pupil, whose name was M. Dutuit, in the latter's beautiful château in Normandy, which contained one of the finest collections of pictures and rare curiosities in all France. It is needless to say that the master was received with enthusiasm by the pupil.

Couture's method of giving a lesson to his pupils was as follows: While they looked on he painted a head from the model, and while he painted made judicious remarks as to the drawing, the color, the light and shade. Some of these heads, dashed off in two hours, are charming. M. Barbedienne, Couture's great friend and admirer, possesses several of them.

In the same collection are numerous drawings, sketches, half-finished pictures, most interesting to those who like to follow the workings of an original genius. Among these is the sketch for his picture, " The Love of Gold." Seated at a table, a man with a fiendish face grasps bags of gold, jewels, and precious stones ; crowding about him, eager for the spoil,

we see beautiful women, writers willing
to sell their pen, artists their brushes,
warriors their valor. Couture's love for
symbolical painting grew with years, developed probably by solitude. In the
very retired life which he led he did not
follow the movement of modern art; he
even refused to see what other artists did,
declining to let them see his own works.
Another of his symbolical pictures, of
which M. Barbedienne possesses a large,
nearly finished sketch, shows us a beautiful young woman seated in a carriage,
whip in hand, driving, instead of horses,
a group of men, — among them a poet, a
warrior, and a satyr-like old lover. I pre-
fer, as a general thing, his simpler works.
Among these I must speak of a little picture representing a boy carrying a tray
on which are glasses full of wine or red
syrup; his head is covered with a sort of
white twisted cloth, and is singularly living and strongly painted.

Couture's love of symbolical pictures
sometimes carried him to the verge of
caricature, as in his series of pictures of
lawyers. He had two pet hatreds, —
lawyers and doctors. In M. Barbedienne's gallery are some very spirited
drawings and sketches of lawyers speaking before the court, or sleeping during
the discourse of their brother lawyers.
As to doctors, he never would allow one
in his house. He was so violent in his
animosity that, when he fell ill, he refused
all medical aid. And his was a terrible
disease, which could not be cured, al-
though his sufferings might at least have
been somewhat allayed.

My poor friend died of a cancer in the
stomach on the 27th of March, 1879.
His loss was a great sorrow to me. We
had been young men together; we had
seen years roll on without bringing any
change in our mutual feelings, and when
one of us experienced some success in

life it was a joy to the other.   For his
talent I had a sincere and profound admiration ; for his strong and manly nature
the greatest sympathy.   He was a friend
in the broadest and best sense of the
word.

CROWNS AND CORONETS.

AT times when I look back upon my long career it seems to me like a tale of olden times, of some mortal guided through forests and over mountains, across seas and plains, by a familiar and capricious spirit. My guide brought me through many a strait, and led me into very unexpected worlds.

As a mere boy in Boston, I was fortunate enough to have as a sitter a very charming and beautiful woman, a leader of fashion of those far-away days, Mrs. Otis, and in an odd, round-about way it was due to her that I painted my first portrait in the world of crowns and coronets.

One day — it was in 1834 — I was working in the Louvre very earnestly from that most adorable of pictures, Correggio's " Mystical Marriage of Saint Catherine."

My impression when I first saw that wonderful gallery was that really the old masters were singularly overrated; that if their fame had not been consecrated by the admiration of several centuries, people would be willing to admit that we modern artists — I dare say I added, we Yankees — were quite capable of painting as well and with more dash and brilliancy. Perhaps many a young and audacious ignoramus has thought and even said as much before and since. When I began to open my eyes, to learn my art, to copy these old masters, I began also to understand that the admiration of centuries was perhaps justified, and that it might require some years of hard work before

I quite came up to Raphael, Vinci, or Correggio.

At any rate, I was that day doing my best, as humbly as I then knew how, to copy the " Marriage," when I suddenly felt that I was no longer alone before my easel. Visitors, English visitors especially, would often, while visiting the Louvre, stop and look at the various copies. These two, husband and wife evidently, pleasant-looking people, were English, and questioned me with interest. Then they moved off with a few kindly words of praise, and I never expected to see them again.

A little later I started for Italy, — a pilgrimage which tempts every young painter, — and naturally I travelled as economically as possible. Generally my journeys were accomplished on foot ; but Italy is a long way off, and I crossed Mont Cenis in the stage-coach. At Alexandria we stopped to rest, and the first people I saw at the inn were the English travellers. To my great surprise and pleasure they recognized me and spoke. In Switzerland they had met a friend to whom, incidentally, they had mentioned the young American painter ; the friend, who was Mrs. Otis, exclaimed : " Why, that must be George ! " And so " George " seemed no longer a stranger to them, and Sir Arthur Brooke Faulkner and his charming wife became the kindest friends and patrons of the unknown American painter.

Sir Arthur and Lady Faulkner travelled in their own carriage. They most graciously offered me a place in it for the rest of the journey; I need not say how eagerly I accepted. In these days of steam we rush through the countries we visit; we do not really see them. Travelling in a comfortable, venerable-looking coach, ingeniously packed with all sorts of portable luxuries, roomy and easy, stopping where and when one chooses, is a delight of which our young people can scarcely form an idea. My enthusiasm for the lovely country in which we found ourselves was enhanced by the delights of a new and warm friendship. By the time we reached Naples it was an understood thing that I should before long go to London and meet my kind English friends.

Events seemed about to shape my career into that of an English artist. Sir Arthur Faulkner, whose position in the London world was a high one, obtained sittings for me from the Duke of Sussex, uncle to the present Queen. This was a splendid opening for a young painter, and I did my very best. The portrait proved successful, and brought me various commissions and some notice.

The Duke of Sussex, who was in those days a middle-aged man, and usually wore a velvet cap on his bald head, was most

amiable and simple. He had made a
left-handed marriage with a lady who
bore the title of Duchess of Inverness.
He was not the only one of the family
who had done so; only he remained
faithful to his chosen mate. She was
a very little woman, just five feet tall,
and he was a man of superb stature, — six
feet four inches. But in that big body
beat a very soft and tender heart. He
was romantic too, and a *preux chevalier*.
He would sing love-ditties to his fair
duchess, accompanying himself on the
guitar. It was a little comical to see,
perhaps, especially on account of his
baldness and portly figure, but I never
felt inclined to smile at this amiable
weakness of his.

Lady Agnes Buller, twin sister of the
Duke of Northumberland, was one of the
most kind and charming of my sitters at
that time, toward 1839. Her conversation was very interesting, but certain

ALEXANDER BARING.
(Lord Ashburton.)

faults of pronunciation contracted in the nursery were still perceptible, in spite of education and intelligence. She was nearly always obliged to repeat the word "picture" to get it right, being always tempted to say "pictur." She envied the children of modest parents who were not shut up with nursery governesses and maids.

Lord and Lady Waldegrave also ordered their portraits. Lady Waldegrave was the daughter of the famous singer, Braham. This delightful tenor's name was really Abraham; but the children of Israel not being yet in odor of sanctity, he thought he might Christianize his name by signing it A. Braham.

One of my pleasantest remembrances of those days was a holiday spent most joyously by my young wife (I had just married), some artist friends, and myself. During a sitting Lord Waldegrave exclaimed: " You ought to visit Strawberry

Hill; it is classic ground." Strawberry Hill was his country-seat at Twickenham, on the Thames. He sent orders to his housekeeper to prepare a good luncheon for us. We started early, taking boat on the river, and I doubt whether a merrier party of young people ever enjoyed a more perfect day. I do not know what the correct servants in livery who waited on us thought of these Americans who filled the superb dining-room with their jokes and laughter; but I am sure they considered that our people are endowed with remarkable appetites. I well remember a certain dish heaped up with a formidable quantity of lamb chops. It left the table quite empty.

Strawberry Hill, which had belonged to Horace Walpole, is beautifully situated, with magnificent gardens sloping down to the river. It was here that Walpole wrote his famous "Letters." Here also, probably, he received many a charming missive from the Marquise du Deffand, the blind old woman so full of wit and charm, whose last romance — a very maternal sort of romance, of course — was woven in honor of the fascinating Englishman.

I remember a very romantic incident of these early years. I painted a small whole-length portrait of the Master of Grant, the head of the clan, in his Highland dress. He was a superb-looking man, and a great favorite with the fair sex. He died suddenly soon after I had finished my work. Two ladies of very high rank ordered a copy of my portrait to be painted secretly and sent to them under lock and key. I never learned the exact truth with regard to these clients of mine, but, naturally, my imagination built up a romance about this mysterious order.

I had thus obtained, at this period of my life, an excellent English connection.

It seemed as though I had but to continue doing my very best to please my aristocratic patrons in order to arrive at a good position and fortune. An incident interrupted my course, and my life was shaped after a very different fashion.

Our Minister at the court of France was then General Cass. He and his family were most kind to me, and remained my very stanch and warm friends to the end. I had painted in 1838 a large portrait of the General. He one day said to the King, Louis Philippe: "I wish your Majesty would allow a young countryman of mine to paint your portrait." The King smilingly gave a vague promise, which, like many royal promises, came to nothing. But when he visited the annual exhibition, which then took place in the Louvre, he examined the General's portrait with interest, and asked abruptly where the young fellow who painted it was at that time. " In

London, Sire." " Tell him that, if he will come to Paris, I am willing to sit to him." Naturally I was soon at his Majesty's orders.

General Cass presented me to the King, and remained during the whole of the first sitting. I remember that the conversation turned especially on Fieschi, who had just been executed. Louis Philippe was not tender on the subject of king-killers, and said: " My dear General, my country-people like to play at being heroes; but I shall let them see that I have the guillotine and the galleys at their service."

Before beginning the portrait I advanced toward the King, so as to take the measure of his face, using a compass for that purpose. One of the courtiers, seeing the gleam of steel in my hand, rushed upon me and pushed me aside. With a smile, Louis Philippe said: " Mr. Healy is a republican, it is true, but he is an American. I am quite safe with him."

The King spoke English most admirably, using it not only correctly, but by no means disdaining familiar expressions. He was perfectly simple, natural, and cordial; full of sympathy with Americans, and remembering his stay in America with pleasure.

With his subjects, however, the King revealed himself, at times, in a most unexpected manner.

On one occasion — it was one of the early sittings devoted to deciding on the attitude — I was making a chalk drawing of the King. While we were trying various views of the head, the *aide de camp de service* who assisted at the sitting, and who doubtless was more accustomed to the life of the camp than to that of the court, threw himself into an exaggerated and theatrical attitude, exclaiming: " Voilà une pose, Sire ! " The King

frowned and said severely: "Monsieur
le général!" The poor General instantly
bowed so low that he seemed to double
up, to collapse, and he humbly muttered:
"Je rétracte, Sire, je rétracte!" It was
an insignificant little incident, but it
showed me clearly what were, inevitably,
the relations of sovereign and courtier.

Louis Philippe grew interested in his
portrait, and his family with him. Madame Adelaide especially, sister to the
King, never missed a sitting, and I saw
familiarly at that time many famous men
whose names are now historical; among
others, Maréchal Soult, then Minister of
War, whom I painted later.

The King's portrait, which belonged to
General Cass, proved a success.[1] Louis
Philippe sent for me one morning and
said: "Mr. Healy, I understand that I
was seen last evening at your Minister's

[1] This portrait, with many others, was burned in the
great Chicago Fire of 1871.

in very good company, — between Washington and Guizot, both painted by you.
Where and how did you copy your Washington?"   I had simply copied it from
an engraving after Stuart's portrait of
Washington, not having the original
within my reach.   The King then told
me that while he and his brother were
in the United States they had seen Stuart
at work on the portrait of Washington
ordered by Mrs. Bingham; during the
sittings Washington had conversed with
the young princes.   The King added:
" And I want you to make me a copy
of that very portrait."

The great difficulty was to know where
to find it.   Louis Philippe said he would
write at once to his Ambassador to London, the Comte de Saint-Aulaire, and
that I was to return in a week's time to
hear the result of his inquiries.   When
I was next summoned to the Tuileries,
the King exclaimed, as soon as he saw

me : " Mr. Healy, we are dished ! The portrait is in Russia, and, under present circumstances, I can ask nothing of the Russian Government. What are we to do? I must have my Washington. I have set my heart on it!" I proposed to copy the whole-length portrait which hangs in Faneuil Hall, in Boston. " No, no ; that is in his military uniform, and I want him as the President of the United States, in his black velvet suit. Will you start for America, and do for the best? I leave the whole affair in your hands. You might copy the portrait which Mrs. Madison cut from its frame in 1814, when the English burned the city of Washington. At any rate, I shall approve whatever you decide to do."

And so it was that the unquiet spirit which all my life has turned my steps now here, now there, sent me back to America. The President, John Tyler, allowed me to paint in the room where the portrait, a rather feeble imitation of Stuart, hung, and still hangs. Later, when I passed through London, I incidentally learned that the portrait which Louis Philippe fancied was in Russia was in reality close to Portland Place, having been purchased by an American, the late John D. Lewis. The trustees of the estate allowed me to finish my copy from it. The King graciously declared himself well pleased with my work, and gave me orders for various other copies, which are still to be seen in the Palace of Versailles.

Among these copies were to be certain historical portraits belonging to the Queen of England. It was not easy to obtain permission to copy in Windsor Castle, but a king's request is always granted. I had the opportunity, while working in what was then called the Waterloo Gallery, — the name was changed later, when Napoleon III.

visited Windsor, — of noticing the dif-
ference of etiquette in the two courts.
Louis Philippe never seemed to consider
it beneath his kingly dignity to be pleasant and kind. Queen Victoria evidently
feared to address an obscure commoner.

I was one day at work copying the
portrait of Lord Bathurst, by Lawrence,
when the Queen and Prince Albert
crossed the gallery and stopped to look
at what I was doing. As she wished for
some details as to the order the King of
France had given me, etc., she turned
to her husband, saying, " Ask Mr. Healy
if," etc.; and Prince Albert put the
questions to me, as though he had been
translating from a foreign tongue. Then
she exclaimed, looking at my copy, " It is
extremely like," and, with the slightest
possible bend of the head, passed on.
I own that my American blood rather
boiled in my veins. But my indignation
did not prevent me from looking very

hard at her Majesty.   I was struck by the delicacy of the features and complexion of the young Queen, and by the extreme elegance of her very handsome husband. This was in 1841.

The Revolution of 1848, which sent Louis Philippe to England an exile, deprived me of my royal patron, and ended my fortune in France.   My English connection was lost, most of my kind friends being dead or dispersed.   During this long period I had gone frequently to the United States, and there had painted many people of note and made many stanch friends; but I had always returned to France.   In 1855 I went to Chicago for the first time, and a year later my family joined me.   It seemed then that I was never likely again to have anything more to do with kings, queens, or princes.

Overwork having brought on a state of nervous prostration, I made up my mind,

in 1866, to return to Europe. As long
as I remained in Chicago I was certain
to do more than my strength would permit, and prolonged sleeplessness was beginning to tell on my health. My family
sailed for France in June, 1866, and I followed just a year later, in time for the
Universal Exhibition.

We spent some years in Rome, where
I worked with more moderation than in
America, and my health became excellent
once more; and it was in Rome that,
very unexpectedly, I again found myself
the painter of princely sitters.

In 1869 the Duke of Nassau visited
the different Roman studios. He wished
to have a portrait of his young niece, the
Princess Oldenburg, then affianced to
the Duke of Weimar. I was fortunate
enough to be chosen; and the Princess,
a fair young girl of about seventeen, gave
me sittings. Her proposed husband
watched the progress of the portrait,

and I was then painfully impressed with the evident want of sympathy which existed between the affianced pair. However, the preparations for the wedding went on. It was on the very eve of the marriage-day that the poor young bride found courage to break it off. The affair — almost unheard-of in the world to which she belonged — made a terrible stir. I must say that my most hearty sympathies were with my gentle, fair young sitter.

But if the Duke of Weimar's visits to my studio were not always perfectly pleasant, another visitor was welcome as sunshine itself. This was a cousin of the young Princess of Oldenburg, the exquisite and charming Princess of Roumania, since queen of that country. She had been sent to Rome for her health, and was greatly enjoying all she saw; enjoying also her freedom from court etiquette, and, I think, maliciously reducing the lady of honor and the chamberlain who accompanied her to the verge of despair.

Before the portrait of her cousin was quite finished, the Princess of Roumania ordered hers, as a surprise for her husband. I painted her dressed in the national costume ; it consisted of a sort of embroidered chemise, with long loose sleeves, an open jacket, a red skirt embroidered in gold, red morocco boots, and a thin tissue veil covering the whole costume, also embroidered in red and gold. The dress was very becoming to her ; her expressive face was almost perfect, the only defect being a rather high forehead. Since those days she has worn her hair according to the present fashion, cut and curled on the forehead, so that this slight defect is no longer noticeable.

Of late years the Queen of Roumania has become well known, and has been much written about in America as well as in Europe. Under the name of Carmen Sylva, she has published poems and novels, meditations and dramatic works, not only in German, her native tongue, but also in French. She has been crowned by the French Academy; and Pierre Loti, the author of " Pêcheurs d'Islande," has written about her with great enthusiasm, if not with perfect discretion. But more than twenty years ago, when she visited my studio, she was scarcely known beyond her own circle and the privileged few who were admitted to her charming presence. She told me, during the long sittings, all about her home life; about " Carl," her husband; about her lovely little baby girl, — so soon, alas! to be taken from her; about her interest in her adopted country, and her desire to do everything humanly possible for the happiness of her people.

She was born Princess of Neuwied, a very small and modest principality on the

PRINCESS ELIZABETH.
(Since Queen of Roumania.)

Rhine, and she was brought up by her admirable mother as simply as any country girl of her neighborhood. Her education, however, was most complete; she speaks English and French as perfectly as her own tongue, and with no vestige of accent. She is an excellent musician, and has a curious talent for miniature-painting and old-fashioned illuminating. All that she does she seems to do with perfect facility; and whatever her task may be, she accomplishes it with as much ardor as though her whole future depended upon its success.

I think that all who have approached the Queen of Roumania will agree with me when I say that no woman was ever more thoroughly a woman, more daintily refined, more genuinely warm-hearted, kind, compassionate, more enamored of all that is pure and noble; and if ever these lines meet her eyes, I rejoice to think that the homage of her American painter may not displease her.

In the course of the sittings the Princess questioned me about the different members of my family. I own to a weakness which I have often tried in vain to overcome. I cannot refrain from talking about my wife and children; and just about that time my first grandson was born, so that he also came in for a share of fond gossip. The Princess seeming interested, — I have said how indulgent she was, — I ventured to say that if she wished to confer a great favor on her painter and dine at his house, he would then present the members of his family to her. "But I should delight to dine with you, Mr. Healy; it would be such fun!" And she really did seem to enjoy the dinner, and the absolute lack of etiquette and ceremony, the hearty pleasure each and all felt in her sweet presence. Only I fear that her lady of honor suffered cruelly. The Princess was so gay, so happy, so delighted with the music of a French "Grand Prix de Rome" from the Villa Medicis hard by, so full of admiration for the beauty of our American country-women, that surely court etiquette, as represented by the worthy lady, must have been at every moment ruffled and exasperated.

I was sincerely most sorry when the portrait was finished and my charming sitter had gone back to her adopted country. But in 1872 I was called to Roumania by the Prince; and I remained at the court some months, painting various portraits of the Prince, of his wife, and their beautiful little daughter, who died shortly after. It was their only child; and they have had none since, to their very great sorrow.

I painted the little girl's portrait, not at Bucharest, but in the mountains, at Sinaia, where the court spends all the warm months. The King has since built

a beautiful palace on the wooded moun-
tain slope; but when I first went to Sinaia
the palace had only been planned, and we
lodged as best we could — not very well,
in truth — in an old monastery, where we
had some difficulty in finding a painting-
room of any sort. But I worked out of
doors a great deal. The little Princess
is represented seated on a rock in the
woods; and her mother, dressed in the
national costume, which she habitually
wears, is seen behind the child, and half
hidden by her.

It was agreed that, in my character of
American, of Republican, I might dispense with all ceremony. The Prince
treated me as kindly as did the Princess,
and I was allowed to work as long and as
quietly as in my own studio, taking my
meals at the royal table when I chose or
having them served in my painting-room.
Both husband and wife would come in
familiarly now and again to see how I

was getting along, and sit down to have
a little talk. On one occasion I remember that the Princess, who was generosity
itself, who was always giving and had
innumerable protégés, showed me her
purse, which seemed very empty, saying:
"Isn't it flat, Mr. Healy? My poor
purse,—it is its normal condition!"

Once again I was to see Roumania.
It was in 1881. I had gone to America,
as I had been accustomed to do every
few years, and was at work in Chicago.
A despatch from the Princess of Roumania reached me at a moment when
several portraits were already begun. The
Prince had been named colonel of a Prus-
sian regiment, and of an Austrian one
also. The rule in such a case is for the
royal colonel to send his portrait to his
new regiment, which is a platonic way
of commanding it. I was requested to
paint both. I excused myself to my
Chicago friends, promised to return soon,

and the next Saturday found me a pas-
senger on a transatlantic steamer. It
was during this visit to Bucharest that
the Prince and Princess became King
and Queen. One day, while I was at
work, the chamberlain came to request my
presence near my royal hosts. I found
them in the throne-room. The Prince
was evidently full of emotion, and so was
his wife. All the members of the Cham-
bers were introduced. They had just
voted the new dignity, and came in a
body to proclaim the result of the vote.
It was a very simple ceremony : the dele-
gates were in their ordinary clothes, and
passed in order before their sovereigns.
The King's hand, which held his written
address, trembled visibly.

But though my sitters were now " Maj-
esties," our relations remained as charming as ever, and it seemed to me that
both, however flattered and pleased they
might be, half regretted the old title.

When I took leave of my hosts, it was with a sad and heavy heart, as though this parting were likely to be the last. I have not seen them since.

During my stay in Rome I painted from memory a portrait of Pope Pius IX. His Holiness, having seen this unfinished work, liked it, and consented to give me a few sittings. This was a great favor, which I highly appreciated. So far I had only seen the Pope, with other strangers, at the Vatican receptions, or from afar when he officiated at St. Peter's, before the events of 1870.

I was introduced one morning into Pius IX.'s library; a pleasant room, simply enough furnished, full of books, the table covered with papers. The Pope was dressed all in white cloth, with scarlet shoes; the hair was white, the face rather pale, with very bright eyes, not incapable of sparkle, for his Holiness knew how to take a joke. He was a pretty good sitter, but somewhat restless, and curious also as to what his painter was about. On one occasion he arose from his seat to look over my shoulder. When I am earnestly at work, I wish my sitters to help me, and do their duty by remaining in the attitude I have chosen. I exclaimed, perhaps a little abruptly: " I beg your Holiness to sit down." The Pope laughed and said : " I am accustomed to give orders, not to receive them. But you see, Mr. Healy, that I also know how to obey," and submissively went back to his chair.

Pius IX. has been dead now many a year. I like to think of the few short sittings he gave me in his cheerful library ; I like to remember his quiet, pleasant talk, his rather Italian-sounding French, his judgments of men and things. One day, speaking of a monk who had left the Church and married, he observed, not without glee: " He has taken his

POPE PIUS IX.

punishment in his own hands." I like especially to feel as though the hours spent in his presence had cast a glow on my later years, as the glorious setting sun behind St. Peter's throws a glamour over Rome, its domes and gardens. I often think, also, of Pius IX.'s gentle reproach to one of my countrymen who, in his American pride, refused to bend before him: " My son, an old man's blessing never did harm to any one."

AMERICAN STATESMEN.

LOUIS PHILIPPE, King of France,
whose sympathies with our country
are well known, ordered me to paint portraits of American statesmen for the
Versailles Gallery. Early in the spring
of 1845 he said, —

"Mr. Healy, I hear that General Jackson is very ill. You must start at once
for the Hermitage."

The Hermitage, General Jackson's
country place, was within twelve miles
of Nashville, Tennessee. I lost no time,
and, somewhat fatigued by the long journey, a good deal excited, a little un-
nerved, too, by the excessive heat, though

it was only the last day of April, I drove to the old hero's door.

General Jackson was suffering from moving dropsy, and for forty days and forty nights had been unable to lie down. He sat in a big arm-chair, propped up with pillows; he was worn out with fatigue and pain, and it was not without difficulty that I was admitted to his presence.

I was so full of my object, so eager about it, that without any preparation I at once made my request. Nature evidently never intended me to be a diplomat. It is not impossible that General Jackson looked upon me as an impostor. At any rate, he answered curtly, —

" Can't sit, sir, — can't sit."

" But, General, the King of France, who has sent me all this way on purpose to paint you, will be greatly disappointed."

" Can't sit, sir, — not for all the kings in Christendom ! "

I could get nothing more from him, and, sick at heart with the disappointment, I bowed and left the irascible old man.

On my return to Nashville I told my story to a friend of mine, who greatly blamed me for having gone directly to the General. Long suffering had made him suspicious of all strangers. He advised me to see young Mrs. Jackson, who happened to be at a friend's house in town that very day. The General had adopted the son of an old friend, Mr. Donelson, who took the name of Jackson. His wife, a young and very charming woman, was a great favorite with the General, and had real influence over him. I went at once, and requested a few minutes' conversation with Mrs. Jackson. She listened to my story, read the King's letter, which I had neglected to show to the General, and promised to do her best. She added : —

ANDREW JACKSON.

" I own that I am not very sanguine. Father is very ill, and it is not easy to make him change his resolutions. Should I succeed, my husband will call at your hotel at eleven o'clock to-morrow, in order to drive you back to the Hermitage."

As can well be imagined, I spent a very restless and feverish night. It was really hard to have taken so long a journey for nothing.

Mrs. Jackson told me afterwards that her task had not been an easy one. At her first words he exclaimed, —

" Can't sit, child. Let me die in peace."

She insisted, used her best arguments — all in vain. Finally she said, —

" Father, I should so like you to sit."

He hesitated, much moved by her earnestness, and, with tears in his eyes, answered, —

" My child, I will sit."

And so, at eleven the next morning,

young Mr. Jackson drove up to my hotel, and it was with a light heart that I took my place at his side.

When the General saw me, he said, —

"Sir, you made a *faux pas* yesterday. You should have shown me the King's letter."

After this things went on very pleasantly and easily. I was admitted into the sick-room as much as I chose, and the General before long seemed to like to have me near him. He was as polite and gracious as he had been unfriendly and curt. But he suffered greatly, and on one occasion he said, —

"I wish I could do you greater justice as a sitter, Mr. Healy."

I assured him that all I asked was that he might forget altogether that he was a sitter.

When the portrait was finished, the different members of the family assembled to see it. All approved it so warmly that the General begged me to make a copy of it for his adopted children. I replied that a copy never had the living look of an original, and that if he could endure the fatigue of further sittings this first portrait should be for him, and I could paint another for Louis Philippe. This he readily agreed to, and I began my second portrait. When it was finished, in its turn, the General said, —

"Mr. Healy, will you remain at the Hermitage long enough to paint a whole-length portrait of my dear child? I request this as a personal favor." The "dear child" was young Mrs. Jackson.

I had just heard that Mr. Clay, whose portrait also the King had ordered, was about to leave Nashville, and I considered that my duty was to try to get a few sittings before he left the city. I shall never forget the impressive way in which the General said, after he had listened to me, —

"Young man, always do your duty; never allow anything to turn you from it."

But I was soon back again. Mr. Clay had already left Nashville, and, owing to an accident to the river boat which he had taken, no one could tell me where he was at that moment. I at once began the portrait. General Jackson watched its progress with eager interest, and on more than one occasion exclaimed, —

"I hope the Lord will spare me long enough to see my dear child's portrait finished!"

I began it early in the week, and on the Saturday afternoon it was almost finished. The old man was much pleased, and looked forward to the following Monday morning, when I was to give the last touches.

I was awakened early on Sunday by a long, pitiable wail. It was the cry of the negro servants, — a sort of cadenced cry;

" Oh, Lord! Oh, Lord! Old massa's dead! Old massa's dead!" The wail was then caught up by the slaves outside of the house, until it spread far and wide, all over the plantation; it was echoed here and there, now sounding close by, now dying off in the distance, always the same: " Old massa's dead! Oh, Lord! Old massa's dead!"

It chilled the blood to hear it, and I remained sadly enough in my room, not daring at such a time to intrude upon the family. However, I soon learned, from two boys, nephews of Mrs. Jackson, that " Grandfather," as they called the General, was not dead; he had had a long fainting-fit, which had at first been mistaken for death, but the end was not far off.

At about six in the evening I went to the door of the sick-room for news. George, the General's black servant, said that his master was very low. I turned to go, when young Mr. Jackson, his face bedewed with tears, came to me.   " Come in," said he; "father is dying."   As I hesitated to disturb them in their grief, he continued: " Please come in.   I wish it."

Ten or twelve persons were already in the room, and all were weeping.   The General was propped up in bed, his head sustained by his great friend, Major Lewis.   Mrs. Jackson was kneeling by the bedside, holding his hand; on the other side of the bed the faithful negro servant stood.

The General seemed unconscious, but suddenly he rallied and looked about him.   He said very distinctly: " Why do you weep for me ?   I am in the hands of the Lord, who is about to release me. You should rejoice that my sufferings are at an end."

These were his last words.   His head dropped, and soon all was over.   On seeing this, his adopted daughter, his " dear

child," fainted, and was carried from the
room.

After leaving the Hermitage, where I
remained some little time after Jackson's
death to finish his adopted daughter's
portrait, I went on to Ashland, Clay's
beautiful country-place near Lexington,
Kentucky. The contrast was great in
every respect. Instead of tears, of suffering, of death, I found happiness, luxury,
and joyous life. Clay, though he had
been a poor boy and a struggling young
man, was at that time one of the most
popular and successful orators and poli-
ticians of the United States. He was
very fascinating in manner, and his
friends took to heart his defeat when he
ran for the Presidency almost as much
as he did himself.

On one occasion he said to me: "Mr.
Healy, you are a capital portrait-painter,
and you are the first who has ever done

justice to my mouth, and it is well pleased to express its gratitude." Clay's mouth was a very peculiar one, thin-lipped and extending almost from ear to ear. "But," he added, "you are an in-different courtier; though you come to us from the French King's presence, you have not once spoken to me of my live-stock. Don't you know that I am prouder of my cows and sheep than of my best speeches?"

I confessed my want of knowledge on the subject, but I willingly accompanied him around the grounds, and admired the superb creatures, saying they would do very well in a picture. I fear that that was not the sort of appreciation he ex-pected, and that I sank very low in his esteem from that moment.

But on another occasion I proved a worse courtier still. His jealousy of Jackson is well known, and the two men formed a very striking contrast. During

HENRY CLAY.

a long sitting he spoke of his old rival, and, knowing that I had just painted the dying man's portrait, he said, —

" You, who have lived so long abroad, far from our political contests and quarrels, ought to be an impartial judge. Jackson, during his lifetime, was held up as a sort of hero; now that he is dead his admirers want to make him out a saint. Do you think he was sincere ? "

" I have just come from his death-bed," I answered; " and if General Jackson was not sincere, then I do not know the meaning of the word."

I shall never forget the keen look shot at me from under Mr. Clay's eyebrows; but he merely observed, —

" I see that you, like all who approached that man, were fascinated by him."

Another time a friend of Mr. Clay, Mr. Davis, speaking of Jackson's proverbial obstinacy, said that one day, looking at a horse, Jackson remarked: "That horse is seventeen feet high." "Seventeen hands you mean, General." "What did I say?" "You said seventeen feet." "Then, by the Eternal! he is seventeen feet high."

Clay would never have sworn to the seventeen feet. He knew how to make himself loved as well as admired. After his defeat by Polk he refused to see any one. It was with great difficulty that his friends obtained his presence at a banquet given in his honor. When he entered the dining-hall, where two hundred guests were assembled, no one present was able to restrain his tears, so popular was Mr. Clay and so great was the disappointment at not having him for President.

It was at a dinner given by Clay at Ashland that I first saw and heard the "negro minstrels." I was delighted with them, and found the performance as original as it was charming. The head of the company, knowing that I lived abroad, asked me whether I thought they would have any chance of success in Europe; they had some idea of trying London. I greatly encouraged the idea, being persuaded that they would succeed admirably. Before I returned to Europe they were all the rage in English society; the Queen was much pleased with their songs; and, naturally, where she smiled, the court and the town laughed and applauded.

Though I had proved so mediocre a courtier, my stay at Ashland was most pleasant, and Mr. Clay was the most courteous and hospitable of hosts. The portrait was successful, and we parted on the best terms possible.

Some time later I was in Washington, where Clay also found himself, and, remembering with pleasure our long talks, I hastened to call upon him. Feeling sure of my welcome, I followed the ser-

vant upstairs, and was near enough to
the door to hear Clay exclaim wearily as
he looked at the card : " What! another?
Well, show him up." But when I entered
he came forward with the sweetest smile
and outstretched hands, saying with an
intonation peculiarly his own : " What!
you here? I thought you were with the
King."

After all, public men, even the best of
them, are obliged to be good actors. It
does not prevent them from being true
friends to the few they really care for.
As to the others, they wish merely to be
popular; popularity is as necessary to
them as the air they breathe.

In September, 1845, I found myself in
Boston; and there I obtained sittings
from John Quincy Adams for the portrait ordered by King Louis Philippe.
John Quincy Adams was then seventy-
eight years of age. Unlike most of his

JOHN QUINCY ADAMS.

predecessors at the White House, he continued to mix actively in politics after his term of office. When he sat to me he was a member of Congress, and was called the "old man eloquent." His conversation was most varied and interesting; so much so that at the time I took a few notes after each sitting, and these, by some chance, escaped destruction, whereas most of my papers were burned in the Chicago Fire or have been lost in my frequent travels.

From his childhood John Quincy Adams had known celebrated personages at home and abroad; his father's name made him welcome everywhere, even before he was appreciated for his own sake. It seemed odd to talk with one who had been in France before the Revolution, whose father had spoken to him familiarly of Voltaire, of Buffon, of the Encyclopédistes, of the French court; who had been at school near Paris, with

Franklin's grandson, somewhere about
the year 1775. In 1845 the sensation
was a strange one; and writing about
these things in 1890 gives one an impression of the long succession of generations holding each other by the hand
until they fade into the far-away past.

One of my sitter's earliest and most
agreeable recollections was that, while
at school with Franklin's grandson, La
Fayette with his young and beautiful
wife visited the boys frequently, and no
doubt brought them sweets from the
Boissier of that day. " I was but a small
boy then," said my sitter, "but I still
remember what a deep impression the
lovely Marquise made on my youthful
imagination."

Later he was able to be of service to
Madame de La Fayette. In the summer of 1792 La Fayette was taken prisoner by the Austrians. This mishap
doubtless saved his life, as, had he been

in Paris during the Terror, he would certainly have been swept away by the revolutionary storm. At that time John Quincy Adams was Minister at The Hague. He there received a letter from the Marquise de La Fayette, who was ruined, and could not join her husband for lack of money. Adams sent her the sum she needed ($1,500), only too happy to be of some service to the wife of La Fayette, remembering also his youthful admiration for the beautiful Marquise. When, in his turn, Robespierre was dragged to the guillotine, a list of intended victims was found among his papers, and Madame de La Fayette's name appeared on that list.

Once more John Quincy Adams saw La Fayette. It was in 1824, a short time before his election as President. La Fayette then visited America, where he was received with great enthusiasm, as was surely quite natural; and the Passy

schoolboy, as Secretary of State, was
able to return the cordial hospitality ten-
dered him at the La Fayette mansion.
John Quincy Adams accompanied the
old hero to Washington. At Alexandria,
during a banquet offered to the " nation's
guest," the mayor, who presided at the
table, received the news of Louis
XVIII.'s death. Should La Fayette be
told of this sad event or not? Adams
was consulted, and, knowing that La
Fayette cordially hated the King, said
he would take it upon himself to break
the news to their guest. He did so, and
La Fayette was obliged to put his hand
up to his mouth to hide a smile.

John Quincy Adams was a most courteous gentleman. The first time he
came to sit I said something about the
annoyance we artists caused celebrated
people. Webster was very frank on the
subject; he compared us to horse-flies on a
hot day, — brush them off on one side, they

settle on the other. Adams smiled, but
said that he was by no means of Webster's
opinion; that he had enjoyed his sittings
to artists on more than one occasion.
He had, perhaps, found that a man busy
with his brush can be a good listener.
I, for one, listened with great pleasure.
Copley had painted an excellent portrait
of my sitter's father, and when I asked
permission to measure the face, as I always do, he observed that he had seen
Copley measure not only his father's
face, but his arms and legs. Then he
spoke of different painters he had known.
He had, as a boy, seen Reynolds, whom
he greatly admired, but who would often
"not let well alone," and spoiled his portraits with over-care. Stuart he had sat
to, though the portrait had to be finished
by Sully after the great artist's death.
He had had many opportunities of studying the old masters in the different galleries. He had seen the Louvre in

Napoleon's time filled with the finest masterpieces, unscrupulously taken from conquered countries.

"But," added he, "there were too many; it was a surfeit of sweets; it was impossible to appreciate each picture seen thus crowded by other pictures. The Dresden Gallery has always seemed to me an ideal gallery."

On the landing outside of my painting-room, John Quincy Adams noticed two busts, that of Voltaire and that of Franklin.

"Sir," said he in his impressive way, "these I should take as representative men of their respective countries. Look at this unquiet skeleton head, so full of satire, of energy, devilishly intellectual, bold in thought, but forced to be wily and full of tricks, capable of violence, however, between two mocking smiles. Voltaire prepared the Revolution which he was not destined to see; indeed, some of his letters seem prophetic. My father saw him when he came to Paris at the age of eighty-four, after having been a kind of voluntary or involuntary exile during the latter part of his life. Public opinion turned at last; he was a sort of god. When he assisted at the first representation of his play, ' Irène,' at the Comédie Française, the whole audience rose and shouted out their enthusiasm. It was too much for the old man; he was killed with kindness. Now look at Franklin's head. It seems a little heavy in comparison, but how solid, how peacefully powerful, how full of reason and that first of qualities, common-sense! A strong-headed Englishman, — for he was an Englishman seventy years of his life."

Then he added: "And yet I love France; I was a boy there; I always went back with pleasure."

He was in Paris during the *cent jours.*

He never spoke to Napoleon, but frequently saw him in public places, at the theatres, at balls, etc. But his sympathies were rather with the Bourbons than with the Bonapartes. While he was President of the United States he frequently saw Joseph Bonaparte, who was quite convinced that he was a much greater man than his brother. His one idea, the object of all his diplomacy and intrigues, was to proclaim his nephew Emperor under the name of Napoleon II., while he himself meant to be an all-powerful regent.

John Quincy Adams was an excellent classical scholar, and while speaking of his favorite authors would grow quite excited, with his eyes cast upward. On more than one occasion I saw him literally trembling with emotion. In those far-away days cold indifference was not yet the fashion. A man did not fear to show the enthusiasm he felt. Mr. Adams

said that he could never, even then, read
the account of the death of Socrates
without tears springing to his eyes. On
one occasion he made a learned comparison between Demosthenes and Cicero,
and confessed that, in spite of the usually
received opinion, his preferences were for
the Latin orator; he *felt* his eloquence
more than that of Demosthenes.

But my great delight was to make him
talk about his early reminiscences of
France and Frenchmen. I remember
an anecdote which he heard from his
father about Buffon. We had been
speaking of the anti-Christian movement
of the last century, of the conviction
among the philosophers that, if the world
was certainly governed by some superior
power, the God worshipped by mortals
did not exist under the form their imagination had given to him. But if
the philosophers between themselves in-
dulged in these bold and subversive doc-

trines, they feared persecution, and never openly expressed them in their writings.

A German who had undertaken a translation of Buffon's works said to him, —

".I see that you constantly use the word ' God.' Do you believe in God?"

" Oh, certainly not. But in France I have to take into consideration the prejudices of the people. In Germany one is free to say what one thinks. Therefore, each time you see 'God' written by me, pray translate it as though it were the word 'nature.'"

This struck me as very characteristic of the state of feeling in France before the Revolution.

While executing the orders of my royal patron, my work brought me in contact with the most celebrated of our public men. It was then that I first conceived the idea of grouping them together in a large historical picture. I chose as my

subject " Webster Replying to Hayne."
The great orator was a magnificent-look-
ing man, with his deep-set eyes, his
superb brow, and his fine massive presence. His, naturally, was one of the
first names on Louis Philippe's list. I
remember that, when I showed his portrait at the court, an impulsive French-
woman asked me whether Mr. Webster
had ever visited Paris. When I assured
her that he had done so, she exclaimed:
" Dieu! et dire que je ne l'ai jamais
vu!"

I was as enthusiastic as the French
lady, but perhaps in a different way.
Webster was the very man for the cen-
tral figure of a large picture. His friends
and enemies, in various attitudes of attention, of admiration, or of indignation, set
him off very well, and in the galleries I
grouped all the prettiest women of the
day, with their big bonnets trimmed
with drooping plumes, and their oddly

made dresses, which in 1846 or 1847 did not seem odd at all.

This was an immense undertaking, which required seven years to accomplish. I painted the picture in Paris; but all the studies, about one hundred and fifty portraits, I made from life. When at last the picture was finished it was exhibited in America, and finally placed in Faneuil Hall, where it is still to be seen.

I painted Webster several times, the last being in 1848 at his country-place, Marshfield. I there made a small picture of our great orator in his hunting-gear; Mrs. Webster, his second wife, is seen in the distance in the doorway. This lady had no children; and as at that time my wife was with me and had a small baby, Mrs. Webster declared that she would go barefooted from Washington to Boston to have such a white, soft, pretty baby of her own. Her husband was very fond of holding the little crea-

DANIEL WEBSTER.

ture in his arms and of playing with it
after a solemn fashion.

Life at Mr. Webster's was very simple
and pleasant; his children by his first wife,
his friends and relatives, made a large
home circle. One of these relatives on
one occasion had Webster as his partner
at whist, and it seems that one can be a
powerful speaker without knowing the
rules of that noble game. Being much
absorbed by thoughts quite foreign to
the cards, Webster forgot to return his
partner's lead, whereupon this gentleman
exclaimed: " Mr. Webster, you play like
the devil's rag-baby!"

It was while I was thus at work in the
United States that I heard of Louis
Philippe's fall; the King of France was
an exile in England. Not only was this
a real grief to me, but, from a worldly
point of view, it was a real calamity.
To fulfil the King's orders I had left an
excellent English connection. Many of

the portraits of American statesmen intended for him were either not finished
or remained on my hands.   I could
scarcely expect that those who had over-
thrown Louis Philippe would think of
keeping his engagements.

However, I continued my work, and
when I had all the materials ready for
my big picture, returned to Paris. I
never regretted the time I devoted to it,
however onerous to an artist such un-
dertakings usually are ; and this one
proved particularly so to me.   But I hold
it an honor to have painted so many of
my illustrious country-people, to have
grouped them about a man of whom all
Americans are so justly proud ; and
whatever criticisms may be addressed to
" Webster Replying to Hayne " as a picture, I can at least affirm that it was
painted with absolute sincerity and regard for nature and truth.   Each head
on that vast canvas is a portrait.

FRENCH STATESMEN.

I HAPPENED to be in London in the spring of 1838, and assisted at the festivities of Queen Victoria's coronation on the 25th of April. It was a very grand sight, and all the different countries sent representatives. Among these, Marshal Soult, who represented his royal master, Louis Philippe, excited most interest and admiration. He was a very rich man, and his government spared nothing to add to the luxury which he was fond of displaying.

But the interest attached to Marshal Soult's embassy was principally due to the way in which he was received by his old enemy, the Duke of Wellington.

The two had been foes worthy of each
other; and their famous campaign, a veritable duel, of 1813–1814, was still fresh in
everybody's memory. Soult had been
accused of knowing that Napoleon had
abdicated, before the battle of Toulouse,
and having kept the news secret. This
was a calumny, and Wellington himself
refuted it. Then Soult's career had
been a very brilliant one, and very characteristic of his time. He entered the
army at sixteen in 1785, and soon won
for himself grade after grade. He was
the youngest of Napoleon's generals on
whom the Emperor conferred the title of
Marshal; he had taken part in most of
the famous campaigns, and assisted at the
terrible siege of Genoa; he was known
as a brave soldier, as an unscrupulous
general too, it must be said, and such
men were highly useful to Napoleon. It
was Soult whom he chose for the Spanish
campaign of 1808; and if ever war was

carried on without much tender mercy,
it was during the five years that Soult
spent in that unfortunate country, bat-
tling against Sir John Moore, quarrelling
with Ney and with the French-imposed
King, Joseph.

After the abdication of the Emperor,
Soult went over to the Bourbons, then
returned to his old allegiance during the
hundred days, and assisted at the battle
of Waterloo. He was banished from
France for three years, but was then
called back and made a peer of France in
1827. Under Louis Philippe he became
Minister of War, and was chosen by the
King to represent him, as we have seen,
at the coronation of the young English
Queen. What Montalembert said of
Talleyrand might have been said of Soult:
" He faithfully accompanied success."

However that may be, it is certain that
he was the observed of all observers in
London in the spring of 1838; and our

minister, Mr. Stevenson, was so struck by his fine presence and grand air that he bade me paint his portrait, if I could get him to sit. This was easier said than done, for he was soon called on to form a ministry, and had no time to give to a young American painter.

However, I wrote to our Minister to Paris, General Cass, on the subject. I was at that time studying Rubens in Antwerp; a highly enthusiastic student, — for to me Rubens is the king of painters. The General answered that he would try to obtain what I asked, and told me, meanwhile, to paint portraits of himself and family. It was through General Cass that, as I have said before, I became known to the King, Louis Philippe, and was employed by him.

On the 1st of March, 1840, Soult's ministry fell, and General Cass presented me to him. We were both invited to

visit his famous gallery of pictures, col-
lected — in reality, stolen — in Spain.
Soult was a rather rough-mannered man ;
one felt he had lived in camps nearly all
his life, and had been accustomed to command. He was very proud of his pictures, and indeed the collection was a
superb one. It contained a number of
paintings by Murillo, Alonzo Cano, and
Ribeira. But the picture which struck
me most was the large Murillo, called
the " Immaculate Conception," and which
has become familiar to every visitor of
the Louvre, since it has been hung in
the Salon Carré. But in those days
only those to whom the Marshal opened
his door were allowed to see this and
his other pictures. After Soult's death
his gallery was sold, and brought nearly
a million and a half of francs; the " Immaculate Conception " alone cost the
Louvre 586,000 francs, — an unheard
of price in those days. It is true that

American millionnaires were not then in the habit of bidding against the Old World amateurs.

As I examined this picture with interest, for I had seen as yet but few works of the great Spanish master, the Marshal said with a somewhat grim smile: " That acquisition saved a man's life." I did not dare to ask for details, but was convinced that those words hid some act of clemency.

In the evening I happened to dine at the same table with an English officer, and, as I was full of my morning's visit, I spoke to him about it.

" Did Soult tell you how the picture saved a man's life ? "

" No."

" Well, then, I will. During the savage Spanish war the French took possession of a monastery. Soult sent for the prior : ' There was a picture over your altar, a

celebrated picture by Murillo. Where
is it?' 'I do not know, Señor General.'
'So much the worse for you. You are
in my power. Try to refresh your memory. If that picture is not brought to me
before sundown, you shall be hanged on
yonder tree.' In the evening the Murillo
belonged to the French General, and the
monk was not hanged : that is how the
picture saved a man's life."

During all the sittings which the terrible Marshal granted me, I could not
help seeing before me the trembling
monk, and the tree on which he came
so near swinging. I was glad to feel that
I should never need Soult's clemency.

I painted a large portrait of the Marshal in his superb gold-embroidered uniform, holding his white plumed hat under
his arm. The picture is now in the Cor-
coran Gallery in Washington.

The Marshal, when he sat to me, was a
little over seventy years of age, and had

attained the highest honors that could be accorded to a soldier. He was made " Maréchal Général," a grade to which only Turenne, Villars, and Maurice de Saxe before him had arrived; he was Duke of Dalmatia, and possessed an immense fortune; whereas his old rival, Ney, not far from the Observatoire in Paris, was shot down like a dog, condemned to death by the very government which before long not only forgave Soult for having served at Waterloo, but covered him with honors. Such is life!

Soult died some ten years after his portrait was finished.

It would have been difficult to find a greater contrast than that which existed between Soult and another of my sitters of that far-off time, Guizot, then one of the most prominent of French statesmen.

Guizot, in his political career, owed almost as much to his defects as to his qualities. No one had greater influence;

M. GUIZOT.

no one was more calumniated, even hated, by his opponents. Cold in manner, exquisitely polite, he was inflexible when he thought himself to be in the right. He believed in liberty, but was violently opposed to popular suffrage. His early childhood had been overshadowed by the terror of the Revolution, — his father, though a Liberal, had perished on the guillotine. He was, by his nature and his principles, eminently fitted to be a member of Louis Philippe's government. When he sat to me, he was Minister of Foreign Affairs.

Guizot was a Protestant, born at Nîmes, one of the towns where religious antagonism has remained violent even in these days of indifference. He was a grandson, on both sides, of Protestant ministers, and had inherited some of their austere and cold eloquence. His early education, after his father's tragical end, was carried on in Geneva, that hot-bed of Protestantism. There he acquired the perfect knowledge of English, as well as of other foreign languages, which proved so useful to him in the early and very hard years of his struggle for daily bread. He had, when a very young man, translated and commented upon Gibbon's " Decline and Fall of the Roman Empire," was a great student of Shakespeare, and an admirer of English ways and English liberty. His biography of Washington so pleased our country-people that some American gentlemen requested me to paint a portrait of the author.

Guizot, who was a highly respected professor, but whose lectures were a little cold and dry, and who as a political man excited such violent antipathies, in private life was not only a man of pure and high principles, but full of tenderness and delicacy. The story of his first marriage is very characteristic.

As quite a young man, he was introduced by an old friend into the most charming and select literary circle. There he constantly heard of a Madame Pauline de Menlan, who was well known as a writer, but he had never happened to meet her. Madame de Menlan fell ill, and she depended on her writings for her daily bread. She received an anonymous letter from some one who begged permission to write her articles until she should be able to resume her work. For some time she was kept in ignorance as to her mysterious correspondent; but at last she insisted that the mask should be removed. She, some years later, became the wife of the anonymous writer, young Guizot, though she was fourteen years older than he. This strange marriage proved perfectly happy; it is true that it lasted but a very short time.

As a sitter, Guizot was not only courteous, but perfectly charming. His conversation was varied and most interesting, and he usually spoke English; all the notes I received from him about his sittings were also written in English. Before beginning the large portrait I made a careful drawing on a canvas, just rubbed in here and there with a little color. This was considered so successful that I left it in its unfinished state, and have kept it ever since.

Guizot was then a man of about fifty-five, in the full strength and vigor of his long life, — he died in 1874, at the age of eighty-six. The head was remarkably fine and delicate, the head of a scholar and of a perfect gentleman.

The name of Guizot invariably calls forth that of Thiers. Friends, or rather allies, at one time, they became, later, political adversaries. Indeed, it is impossible to imagine how two natures so different in every way, so opposed even, could sympathize with each other. Yet

both were born in the same southern
town of Nîmes; but Guizot belonged to
the Protestant South, which is as different as possible from the real French South.
Thiers had all the mobility, the ready wit,
the brilliancy of his native place; and
these made of him, in spite of his peculiar, small, and high-pitched voice, an
excellent orator, capable not only of con-
vincing his hearers but of carrying them
away with him. His rival's unbending
and cold determination seemed to Thiers
the very reverse of what is expected of a
political man. Yet the career of each
seemed to pursue about the same lines;
each, in his way, was always before the
public, and each followed the other's
doings with the uneasy interest one always feels in a rival. Some one said of
Thiers, who was just ten years younger
than his fellow-townsman: "So long as
Guizot is not buried, Thiers will always
fancy that he has ten good' years before

him!" Both lived to be old, but Thiers did not have his full ten years of grace.

I did not paint Thiers' portrait till he was an old man, in 1875. Our minister to Paris was then Mr. Washburn, for whom I felt great friendship. He had been, during the war of 1870-1871, a very important personage. Representing an entirely independent country, he was naturally designed to take the place of other ambassadors whose stay in Paris had become impossible. He had thus become acquainted with all the leading men of the day, and commissioned me to paint portraits of them. In that way, by degrees, he acquired an historical gallery perhaps unique of its kind.

Thiers was the first who was requested to sit to me. He was then a white-haired man, very active, very bright, very decided in his manner; his eyes shone and sparkled behind his spectacles; his tuft of white hair, amusingly exaggerated

LOUIS ADOLPHE THIERS.

in all caricatures, was odd, but in no way
ridiculous; his small body had remained
very supple, and he made the most of
every inch of his diminutive stature.
His conversation was very varied, full of
anecdotes, and he was fond of talking.
When he did not feel inclined to con-
verse, he at once fell asleep. He was an
extremely early riser, and would often
astonish people by appointing five or six
o'clock in the morning for a business
interview; but he snatched many a five
minutes' doze during the day.

Indeed, to the uninitiated this peculiar-
ity, which had extended to his wife and
his sister-in-law, was rather startling.
The mansion of the Place Saint-Georges
was open to friends every evening; but a
visitor, if he happened to drop in too
soon after dinner, before the greater
number of guests had arrived, would not
unfrequently find Madame Thiers fast
asleep on one side of the fireplace, Ma-

demoiselle Dosne, her sister, on the
other, and the master of the house taking a quiet nap, almost hidden in a big
armchair by the table.   And the nods
with which a remark was received were
not always nods of acquiescence.   On
more than one occasion I have retreated
on tip-toe, fearing to disturb by my presence the repose of the venerable trio.

But if, when the drawing-room was full
of interesting guests, the ladies sometimes continued their peaceful repose,
Thiers himself was wide awake and in
his real element.

He had a method which might be rec-
ommended to many a public man.   He
never wrote out his speeches, but, like
actors who rehearse frequently before
appearing in public, he would try the
effect of his future speech on his friends ;
he in that way became perfectly familiar
with his subject, could begin anywhere,
feared no interruptions, was quite master

of himself ; and if perchance some ora-
torical effect on which he had counted
did not succeed, he immediately abandoned it and tried another. Often, before speaking in the tribune, Thiers had
already made his speech ten or twelve
times.

When he sat to me, he had fallen
from power, but he was considered the
" occult leader " of France. He was
consulted, honored, feared. He could
not resign himself to inactivity after
having for so long a time and under so
many forms of government directed the
political world. He grouped about him
as many as possible of the distinguished
political or literary men of the day.
Gambetta — the " dauphin," as people
called him — was a constant visitor.
Thiers appreciated the talent of the
young dictator, appreciated also his
ardent patriotism, and the two often consulted together as to the best means of

maintaining the Republic and of combating its enemies. M. de Remusat, whose perfect manners made him a welcome guest everywhere, and whose noble life was known to all, was one of Thiers' oldest and most faithful friends. Mignet, the historian, was about Thiers' age, and, living in the same part of Paris as his old friend, was nearly always to be seen, of an evening, in the salon of the Place Saint-Georges. Barthélemy Saint-Hilaire was another constant guest. Occasionally M. Jules Simon went to pay his court to Thiers, who had won for himself the glorious title of "libérateur du territoire."

Thiers was very friendly to our country, and he gave me, during one of the sittings, a pleasant proof of this friendliness. Some of his friends assisted at this sitting, and the talk happened to fall on the dramatic author, Sardou : —

"We came near having a quarrel,

Sardou and I," said the ex-President.
" As long as I was in power I absolutely
refused to allow ' L'oncle Sam ' to be
represented on the boards of a Paris
theatre. I considered it a libel, an un-
warranted satire levelled at a country
which had every right to our sympathies."

" At any rate," observed one of his
friends, " it is a satire which since that
time has had great success and brought
in large sums of money to its author."

Thiers turned to me, and said with
charming courtesy, —

" C'était payer fort cher des portraits
bien peu ressemblants" (It was paying
dear for most unfaithful portraits).

In 1877, just before the death of
Thiers, I went to Berlin and, still at the
request of Washburn, painted a portrait
of Bismarck. It was rather a curious
sensation to have before me as a sitter,
after Thiers and Gambetta, their terrible
adversary. With me, the Prince felt at

liberty to forget all about politics, all about vexing questions. I lived with him and his family, ate at their table, heard their familiar talk. It seemed hard to imagine that this excellent husband and father, this man who seemed cut out to be a country gentleman, to hunt and live a jolly careless life, should be the Bismarck whose name evoked such bloody and cruel memories. " Ah ! Mr. Healy," said he on one occasion, " I was born with a kind heart, well disposed toward others; but men have made me hard. Instead of being Chancellor I ought to have been the Pope of Rome." In the course of conversation, the Prince spoke, not only with consideration but with admiration, of Thiers. Alluding to the fortress of Belfort, which, by dint of energy and excellent diplomacy, Thiers had saved for France, Bismarck said: " He is a good patriot."

On my return to Paris I called on

Thiers, and had great pleasure in re-
peating to him what the great German
had said. It was, I think, peculiarly
pleasant to the French statesman.

An anecdote to finish. It is perfectly
authentic, told by Thiers himself.

I said that when I at last obtained sittings of Soult in 1840 he had fallen from
power. His successor was Thiers. The
King, Louis Philippe, knew that the Marshal clung to power, and that his fall
would be bitter to him. But all was arranged beforehand; the future ministers,
with Thiers at their head, were assembled
at the Tuileries, while in the next room
Louis Philippe broke the news to Soult.
The interview took a long time, and the
new ministers were not without some
apprehension. " Finally," here I quote
Thiers, " the door was opened just
enough to allow the King's head — you
know that queer pear-shaped head — to
pass, and he whispered to us: ' A little

patience, gentlemen, just a little patience, — we are weeping together!'"

It was in 1877 that I painted my portrait of Gambetta, intended for Mr. Washburn.

Gambetta was also from the South; indeed, it seems as though the heat of the Southern sun were necessary to ripen eloquence. He was born at Cahors, a picturesque little town, and never lost his rolling accent, which so adds to the force of a fine tirade. It has always been said that Mirabeau would not have been quite Mirabeau without his accent, and that had a Northern man said the famous "Nous sommes ici par la volonté du peuple, et nous n'en sortirons que par la force des baïonnettes!" history would scarcely have recorded it as it has done. Gambetta has often been compared to Mirabeau for his impetuous eloquence, and his influence on the masses. He was not a correct speaker, he

LÉON GAMBETTA.

cared but little for academic elegance,
and his speeches, published since his
death, hardly give an idea of the tre-
mendous torrent of the spoken words.
The voice was powerful, the gestures
appropriate, and above all, he was so
much in earnest, so carried away, himself, by the passion of the moment that
it was impossible to resist " ce diable
d'homme ! "

From his youth, when, as a poor student of law, he came to Paris, he almost
at once took position as a leader. His
young comrades flocked about him ; he
never doubted that he was destined to
do great things; they never doubted it,
either. It is said that Thiers, as a mere
boy, was wont to say, " When I am in
the ministry, I shall do so and so ; "
and what would have seemed ridiculous
boasting in another was quite natural
with him, no one ever thought of
smiling. Not more than Thiers, did

Gambetta doubt the future. Only his future was destined to be a very short one; he died at forty-three years of age.

Personally, Gambetta was much courted, and his friends loved him dearly. He had that rare gift, personal magnetism. And yet he was full of faults; he never could rid himself of certain rough habits, contracted in his youth; accustomed especially to men's society, he was at times a little coarse, loud-voiced, and in the habit of putting himself very much at his ease wherever he happened to be. I remember that my first impression of the great orator was not a favorable one. It was in 1875, at a well-known political lady's house, where all the men prominent in the republican party assembled regularly. Gambetta had spoken that day at the Chamber with even more than ordinary success; enthusiasm was at its height, and he was the great man of the day.

He came late, and though usually when he went into society he took refuge in the smoking-room, where, surrounded by his usual court, he could drink beer and talk with perfect freedom, that evening he went into the drawing-room. Seated, or rather half-reclining on a lounge, he was immediately surrounded by the prettiest and most charming young women of the society, who, seated about him, seemed almost in adoration before this popular idol. It would have been difficult for any man to remain, in spite of such flattery, quite simple and unspoiled. With my American ideas on the subject of feminine dignity, I own that this little scene shocked me greatly.

But these were, after all, but small defects. When one thinks of the immense popularity of this young man after the disastrous war of 1870–1871, of the way in which power seemed to be thrust upon him, how easy it would have been to

usurp more than the surname of " Dictator " which his adversaries gave him, and
with what proud and pure patriotism he
refrained from making use of the dangerous weapon he held in his hand, one can
but admire him. With many faults he
had one great virtue, — he loved his
country above all things, more than
himself.

As a sitter, he was particularly simple-
mannered and pleasant. He had real
sympathy with America and Americans,
though he had but few opportunities of
meeting my country-people, and he did
not know a word of English. But with
the men of republican convictions who
grew up during the Empire, America was
a sort of rallying word, and I fear that in
the fancy of many an enthusiastic youth
our country was endowed with more stoi-
cal and pure republican virtues than it
could honestly lay claim to. Spartan simplicity is not perhaps our invariable rule.

When General Grant made his tour through Europe, accompanied by his wife and son, knowing that I was acquainted with Gambetta, he expressed the desire of meeting him. I was fortunate enough to have both these great men at my table. If in the smoking-room Gambetta sometimes allowed himself a certain license, in the presence of General Grant and our other friends, it would have been impossible to imagine a better-mannered, more courtly gentleman. He had evidently determined to make a good impression on the celebrated American General; and certainly he succeeded.

The contrast between the two was a very striking one, — Grant, with his characteristic square American head, full of will and determination, his reddish beard sprinkled with gray, his spare gestures, and his taciturnity; and this Frenchman, with his Southern exuberant manner, his gestures, his quick replies, the mobility of expression on his rather massive face. Some premature white was seen in his very black hair and beard; his one eye was full of fire and expression (the other was a glass eye); his person was somewhat unwieldy, but his movements were rapid and easy. They seemed typical representatives of the two nations. On one point, however, they were quite alike. If Gambetta spoke no English, Grant knew not a word of French. But they said very flattering things to each other, which one of my daughters was kept busy in translating; each was delighted with the other. Indeed, in order to disagree, the first requisite is to dispense with an interpreter.

In another trifling matter the contrast was very strong. Grant confided to Mrs. Healy that all these grand dinners at which he assisted day after day, with their innumerable dishes and varied wines, wearied him to death, and that he would give them all for a good honest dish of pork and beans. In the midst of his sparkling talk and charming amiability, the Frenchman found means of studying the *menu* with a connoisseur's attention ; his choice fell upon the most refined, truffled, and unhealthy of the dishes. Seeing my daughter, who sat by him, take a slice of roast beef, he gently reproached her for not choosing such or such a delicacy instead.

His fondness for the good things of this world was destined to play Gambetta an ugly trick. He would certainly have died young, for he was a man who spent his strength in overwork and in pleasure too; but his liking for truffles and highly spiced dishes helped, it is said, to hasten his end.

When the news of his death spread abroad, he was mourned most sincerely; and even his political enemies — and they were numerous — were bound to pay their tribute to this very remarkable man, this great and noble patriot. I have always been happy to look back upon the days when he sat to me and talked in his free, simple, and charming way.

My portrait of M. Jules Simon was painted in 1889, and exhibited in the Salon of 1890. It is intended for the Newberry Library of Chicago, to which institution I have determined to leave a number of my historical portraits.

It is difficult to speak of a man still living, even though he belongs partly to history, and few men are more difficult to define than M. Jules Simon. He has been from his youth a stanch republican, and refused to take the oath required of all public functionaries, when Napoleon III. came into power. M. Jules Simon was then professor at the Sorbonne, and well known for his eloquence. He had not a penny of his own, and did not hesitate to lose his place, for conscience sake, though he had a wife and children. He is known to be most scrupulously honest; yet he has had bitter enemies, even in his own party. He has reputation, he is admired, and yet has never attained that highest rank which seemed his due. He is known to be clever, perhaps too clever, in his dealings with men, using a sort of diplomatic *finesse* when a straightforward simple course might suffice. He has not a very exalted idea of humanity in general, and does not hide his feelings quite enough, doubtless. Had men known how to appreciate him as he certainly deserved to be appreciated, his opinion of human nature might have been modified.

Born in Brittany in 1814, he came to Paris as a very young man, penniless, but determined to make his way in the world.

He entered the École Normale, which has formed so many eminent professors, historians, political men, and men of science.

One of the leading philosophers of that day was Victor Cousin, a man who, though he exercised real influence over his contemporaries, has been severely judged by the present generation. Young Simon became his secretary, and had every occasion of studying him. Some years ago M. Jules Simon published a little book on his old master which is a perfect gem, and one of the most amusing biographies I have ever read. It is a superb, whole-length portrait of the old philosopher, with his handsome face, his elevated theories, his utter heartlessness, his talent for making use of young men, and, while seeming to do them a favor, extracting from them their brains, their time, their very life. Yet the outward forms of respect are scrupulously ob-

served. The wit — and it is full of wit —
is veiled and softened and made exquisite
by its very discretion.

Perhaps one of the secrets of M. Jules
Simon's want of popularity is his well-
known humor, his satirical vein, his power
of portraying people, — at times even of
caricaturing them. Those who are most
willing to laugh at the grotesque likeness
of a friend are rarely willing to sit for
their own portrait.

As a conversationalist, M. Jules Simon
is justly celebrated. When he suddenly
remembers some anecdote, some trait of
this or that celebrated man whom he
once knew, — and there are few great
men whom he has not known, — his
whole aspect changes, he then forgets
that he is an old man; the eyes brighten,
the drooping figure straightens, the head
is no longer held a little on one side,
the whole face is lighted up. The voice,
a little weak and high-pitched, is at first

almost feeble, and then grows stronger as the interest increases. This is true not only of his conversation but of his public speeches.

His anecdotes about Cousin are mostly well known; but here is one which does not figure in his biography, and which M. Jules Simon tells with peculiar gusto.

Some years ago, at the funeral of a member of the French Academy, all the Academicians, according to custom, assisted at the ceremony in their gala costumes, — green embroidered dress-coat and sword at the side.

One of these gentlemen, as he climbed into a mourning-carriage where M. Jules Simon had already taken place, got the sword between his legs and exclaimed: " When one is not accustomed to this sort of thing, it is singularly embarrassing !" " Yes," answered M. Simon, " but it is a more useful instrument than one is apt to think." As he was pressed to say how and under what extraordinary circumstances an Academician's sword could be of use, he began in his peculiar, high-pitched voice : —

" When I slaved for Cousin, he generously gave me for my work eighty-four francs (not quite seventeen dollars) a month. Toward the end of the fourth week the obtaining of a dinner was a harder problem to solve than any of the metaphysical questions I worked over during the day. On one occasion, my purse being as flat as any of the speeches we are to make presently, I, toward the end of the afternoon, went to pay a visit to my old master. As the door opened, a delicious odor of roasting chicken greeted me. Never did perfume seem more enchanting. Cousin was fond of a good talk, and I, in a Machiavelian spirit, led the conversation up to his most cherished philosophical hobbies. I never showed greater deference for the great man, or greater admiration. I called to my aid all the wit I could command. I was eloquent; I was full of passion, of fire. The delicious fragrance which pursued me even into the library inspired me. My success was moderate. At times Cousin, carried away by his favorite topics, seemed to forget everything else. But, on the whole, he was uneasy; he moved in his chair, played with his paper knife, like a man who finds that the visit he is forced to submit to is very long indeed. Finally he rose, and I was forced to rise also; he opened his library door, and there was nothing for it but to allow myself to be turned out. But in the antechamber the odor was so strong that it gave me the courage of despair, and I exclaimed: 'Monsieur Cousin, I have not a penny left and I am hungry!' Cousin hesitated; no man was more lavish of words, none less so of everything else. But even his heart was

touched. Impulsively he took my arm,
exclaiming: ' Allons le débrocher!'
And together we went into the kitchen.
There I saw a fine chicken, just roasted
to a rich golden hue, and spitted — on
my master's Academic sword. You see
that the weapon can be of some use,
after all!"

MEN OF LETTERS.

WHEN I was in London as a very young man, in 1838, the great naturalist Audubon visited the British metropolis. He was received with delight by all the American colony, and I naturally took part in that demonstration of enthusiasm.

Audubon was of French extraction, born in New Orleans, but his family for two generations had been American citizens. He was a very simple man, a little rough in appearance, with long shaggy black hair, and the most piercing eyes I ever saw, — real eagle eyes.

I called upon him and asked him to sit to me. He assured me that though he was greatly flattered, he could not

JOHN JAMES AUDUBON.

possibly spare the time. He had come
to London to bring out his big book on
birds, and was too much absorbed by this
work to think of sitting. Then, as he
was a kindly man, he added: " I have
but my evenings to offer you."

Doubtless he thought to escape me in
that way. But artists are persevering;
I am peculiarly so.

" The very thing, my dear sir! I shall
make an original portrait by gas-light."

The great man was caught, and very
graciously accepted his defeat.

I painted him in the costume he wore
when he went in search of his birds, — a
sort of backwoodsman's dress. The portrait was a curiously bright one, as though
it had been painted in full sunshine.

In the course of conversation Audubon
discovered that I was in love with a young
English girl; he became at once very
friendly and communicative, assuring me
that a good marriage was the only real

happiness one could hope for in life. And he told me how he had married a governess, as poor as he then was himself, and how absolutely happy they had both been, in spite of all the material difficulties they had encountered. High culture and a loving heart are the only treasures that are not subject to ruin. He found me a willing listener, and easily convinced of the truth he so eloquently preached.

This portrait is now the property of the Boston Ornithological Society. I took it to America with me some years after I painted it. On that occasion a young brother artist residing in Paris asked me to take over some of his works and to dispose of them, if I could. These were not quite according to the taste of our puritanic countrymen. One, in particular, represented a young woman at her toilet, who, not having advanced much in the process of clothing herself, wore

nothing but a small cap. A good Bos-
tonian, to whom I praised this little picture, said : " No doubt it is very fine, Mr.
Healy ; but my wife would not allow me
to hang it in our bedroom, and I should
not dare to let it be seen in my parlor ! "
I finally determined to dispose of the
pictures by tickets, and, to add to the
interest of the raffle, I put in with
them my portrait of Audubon. As it
happened, one of my own tickets won it.
I then wrote to Mr. Bradley, of Boston,
who had proved one of my best friends,
telling him how the portrait still belonged
to me and begging him to accept it.
Later, with my ready consent, he gave
it to the Ornithological Society, where I
believe it still hangs.

Early in the century, two school-boys
were playing together. One of them, in
fun, threw a crust of bread at his companion, destroying one of his eyes. The
other grew to be very weak ; and the boy,

though he did not become entirely blind, and was able to the last to direct his steps, was still cut off from the usual pleasures of an active life. Fortunately he was able to devote himself to study, and, with the help of secretaries, to historical labors.

That boy was our great Prescott.

In 1843 I called on him and asked him to sit to me. I found him in his handsome study, where subsequently I spent many very pleasant hours, in the company of all the cultivated men of the day. Prescott's was one of the most hospitable and agreeable houses of Boston.

To me, our celebrated historian's life is a proof that happiness is in us, and depends, on the whole, but little on outward circumstances. This almost blind man was serenely content; perhaps one of the happiest among my numerous sitters. His time was fully occupied; his work was a delight to him, and he never allowed small difficulties to stop him on his way. In order to write his Spanish histories, or those of the conquests, he was forced to become familiar with the old Spanish works. His secretary, without knowing a word of the language, read all these to him as best he could, and Prescott managed to understand the meaning of the ill-pronounced words.

It must be added that, had Prescott been forced to fight the hard battle of life, to struggle for his daily bread, the case would have been a very different one. But he possessed a sufficient fortune; no weary material cares forced themselves between him and his work. Reputation came rapidly; he was honored and respected by all; he had many and very warm friends.

No man was more worthy of success than he; no one enjoyed that success with more moderation; no one perhaps ever had fewer enemies or excited less ill-

feeling and envy. It seemed almost as
though his infirmity protected him even
from the naturally envious.

President Pierce, somewhere about
1847, requested me to paint a portrait
of Hawthorne, who was a great friend of
his. As I had vast admiration for Hawthorne's talent, — his genius one might
say, — no commission could have given
me more pleasure.

The novelist was then about forty
years of age, a most striking-looking
man, a little after the fashion of Webster:
heavy black eyebrows overshadowed the
eyes; he had a shock of black hair and
a heavy moustache. One might have
fancied this strong, characteristic head
betokened a resolute and bold nature.
Hawthorne had doubtless great energy,
but I never met man or woman so painfully, so irremediably, timid. This excessive and shrinking sensitiveness rendered
the first sittings very trying, not only to

the model, but to the painter. Each
time the great writer caught my eye —
and of course this happened constantly —
he would shrink, grow crimson, and look
the very picture of misery.

After a few sittings, however, this wore
off, and, strange to say, the presence of
Mrs. Healy, instead of augmenting his
uneasiness, seemed rather to calm it.
He seemed pleased with her appreciation of his works; and when it was proposed that she should read aloud, he
willingly agreed. After this, the sittings
ceased to be a torture to both of us. I
remember that it was one of Bulwer's
novels to which, during the sittings, he
listened with evident satisfaction.

One of the problems my wife and I
puzzled over most, was how so timid a
man ever made up his mind to propose
to any young lady and marry her. But
he had then been married for some years,
and a red-headed boy of his — who since

has made a name for himself in the
world of letters — came to my studio to
see his father's portrait.

When the first shyness had worn off,
Hawthorne told us, in his quaint interesting way, of his early married life. He
and his wife, like ourselves, had begun
housekeeping very modestly — and were
none the less happy for that! The great
question with them was how to furnish
their small house; for in America no
one could have begun life as we did, with
a painting-room and a bedroom next to
it. Mrs. Hawthorne was not only active
and intelligent, but somewhat of an artist
besides. She caused the furniture to be
made of common white wood, of the
cheapest kind; and soon tables and
chairs, sideboards and beds, were all gay
with painted flowers and leaves, birds
and insects. The great man, not without pride, said that when their friends
came to see them, their first exclamation

was: "Where did you get that pretty furniture?"

Perhaps later, when success had fairly come, and with it the possibility of having a well-furnished house, Mr. and Mrs. Hawthorne more than once thought with regret of their white wood tables and chairs!

The same year that I painted Hawthorne, Ticknor—or "Spanish Literature" as he was usually called—sat to me for my big picture of "Webster Replying to Hayne," in which he figures prominently.

The Ticknors lived very handsomely in a big Boston house, and the library was perhaps the largest and most complete private library in America. This hospitable house was open to all cultivated Americans, and a centre for the distinguished foreigners who visited our country.

When Thackeray came to America and gave his successful lectures on the

" Four Georges " he was Ticknor's constant guest. The two were great cronies, which did not prevent them from disagreeing on many a point, each defending his opinion with rare energy. Ticknor was a small, combative, eager man. Thackeray towered above him, but did not always come off victorious in the wordy combats, though he had quick wit with tongue as well as pen, and generally managed to have the last word or joke.

On one occasion, when the discussion had been particularly lively, — it was some point of history which was the bone of contention, — Thackeray, suddenly putting a hand on each shoulder of his friend and looking down upon him, exclaimed, —

" It would never do for two such broken-nosed old coves as we are to fall out and quarrel."

A general laugh ended the dispute. Thackeray, when a boy, had his nose broken by accident; whereas Ticknor, by a freak of nature, had a queer little pug nose that had a broken look. After that, instead of " Spanish Literature " he was usually called " the broken-nosed old cove."

Since I have alluded to the great English novelist, I must speak of two very characteristic meetings with him, though he was never a sitter of mine, and though certainly I could scarcely boast of having been his friend. These two meetings revealed, in the first place, his known weakness for titles and high-born people; the other his really kind nature, which he was wont to hide with a sort of curious false shame.

One day, in Paris, I met Thackeray in the Rue de la Paix. "What! you here, Healy? I thought you were in America!" I replied that I was then working close at hand, in number 15 of the street we stood in, and that if on the following

Thursday he had a moment to spare, I should be glad to show him my work. "Ah! Thursday, — very well." At the time appointed he called upon me and was, for him, most amiable.

In the course of conversation, he said: "So we are to meet this evening;" and as I seemed bewildered, he added : " Why, yes — Thursday evening — did you not say that we were to meet at Lord Holland's?" "No," answered I, " I am not invited." "Ah! really, good afternoon!" And almost instantly he left the place, evidently quite disgusted at having lost his time with a man whom Lord Holland had not seen fit to invite!

Some years later I called on him in Boston, and he received me with a sarcastic smile, assuring me that he felt exceedingly honored that I should condescend to think of a poor man of letters, like himself. I answered with great seriousness : " Mr. Thackeray, you quite

mistake the motive of my visit. It is not
the man of letters I have come to see,
it is the man simply, — the man who
cheered the last days of a poor young
fellow, Cook." Instantly his manner
changed. " Ah! you knew Cook!" And
he spoke feelingly, as though sarcasm had
not become with him almost a second
nature.

Cook, a young American painter whom
I had known in Paris, very poor and
friendless, fell ill, and having no other
resources was compelled to go to the
hospital. There I found him, not only
very ill, but in terror of the doctors, who,
according to him, made use of him for
all sorts of surgical experiments. " If
you can't get me out of this hell, I shall
die of fright." I immediately started a
subscription among the artists, who are
never deaf to such appeals, with the result that Cook was taken to the country.
He had a cheerful room in a farmhouse,

and a garden where he could enjoy every
ray of sunshine. A kind nurse took care
of him ; and a more grateful, happy creature I never saw. He died, in spite of
every care ; but at least his end was not
made horrible by terror. All he could
say was : " I am happy, I am so happy ! "

His most constant visitor was Thackeray, who watched with him night after
night, and cared for this young stranger
as though he had been of his own blood ;
and I am very sure that in order to
give the dying man one bright hour, the
celebrated author would have refused
even a duke's invitation.

My acquaintance with our great poet
Longfellow began many years ago, and I
never went to Cambridge without calling
on him in his delightful mansion, so full
of the memories of our great war. My
first portrait of Longfellow, painted when
he was still young, belongs to his pub-
lishers, Messrs. Ticknor and Fields. In
1870 I again painted him.

LONGFELLOW AND DAUGHTER.

I was then settled in Rome, and Longfellow, with his daughters, spent some
months in the Eternal City. He was
then a splendid-looking man, with perfectly white hair and beard. His eyes
were bright and expressive. I painted a
group of himself with one of his daughters, a very young girl with golden hair;
the contrast was a very telling one.

In my studio the picture he looked at
most often was a large portrait of Liszt
seated at his piano. I had recently
painted it, and I told the poet how, during the sittings, Liszt had played, for
hours at a time. I showed him casts I
had had taken of the musician's hands;
and these greatly interested him, for they
were extraordinary, — thin, nervous, and
well shaped; revealing much of the man's
passionate, unquiet, earnest nature.

Liszt in those days — L'abbé Liszt, as
he liked to be called: he had taken minor
orders — had his lodging in an old con-

vent close to the Forum. Longfellow expressed a desire to see the great musician; and as I had remained on good terms with my sitter, I asked permission to present the American poet to him.

One day, toward sundown, we drove together to the old monastery, and rang at Liszt's private entrance. It was already quite dark in the vestibule, the door of which was opened by means of an interior cord. No servant was visible. But the abbé himself came forward to greet us, holding a Roman lamp high up, so as to see his way. The characteristic head, with the long iron-gray hair, the sharp-cut features and piercing dark eyes, the tall, lank body draped in the priestly garb, formed so striking a picture that Mr. Longfellow exclaimed under his breath: "Mr. Healy, you must paint that for me!"

Our visit was most agreeable, for, when he chose, no man was more fascinating

FRANZ LISZT.

than Liszt. He played for us on his
fine American piano, with which he was
delighted; then he showed us over his
bachelor establishment, which was by no
means the cell of an austere monk; and
evidently wished to make a good impression on his illustrious visitor.

Taking advantage of this amiable dis-
position, I told him how much we had
both been struck by his appearance as
he came toward us, light in hand. He
willingly consented to sit, and I made a
small picture, as exact a reproduction as
possible of what we had seen, and which
gave great pleasure to Longfellow.